Surviving Hitler's Army

A Family Memoir

Ingrid Dolezal Bens

Surviving Hitler's Army: A Family Memoir

Ingrid Dolezal Bens

Copyright© 2022 by Ingrid Bens

All rights reserved.

No part of this publication may be reproduced, stored in a retrieval system, or transmitted in any from or by any means electronic, mechanical, photocopying, recording, scanning, or otherwise, except as permitted under the United States Copyright Act, without the prior written consent of the author.

Limit of Liability/Disclaimer of Warranty: While the publisher and the author have used their best efforts in preparing this book, they make no representations or warranties with respect to the accuracy or completeness of the contents of this book and specifically disclaim any implied warranties of merchantability or fitness for a particular purpose. No warranty may be created or extended by sales representatives or written sales materials. The advice and strategies contained herein may not be suitable for your situation. You should consult with a professional where appropriate. Neither the publisher nor author shall be liable for any loss of profit or any other commercial damages, including but not limited to special, incidental, consequential, or other damages. Readers should be aware that Internet websites offered as citations and/or sources for further information may have changed or disappeared between the time this was written and when it is read.

ISBN: 978-0-9970970-3-0

LCCN: 2022909596

This is dedicated to my parents, Heinrich and Theresa Dolezal who demonstrated incredible courage and resilience and who sacrificed greatly to bring their children to a safe haven. It is also dedicated to all those who continue to suffer the horrors of war.

You remind us that peace and freedom from tyranny are always worth the struggle.

World War II by the Numbers

- A total of 75 million people died in Europe and Asia *
- An additional 25 million people were wounded
- Over 50% of all fatalities were women and children
- Approximately 30 million Russians were killed: 10 million were soldiers, 9 million were children
- Total soldiers: Russia 12.5 mil, USA 12.365 mil, Germany 10 mil
- Approximately 400,000 British military personnel were killed
- Approximately 417,000 American military personnel were killed
- Approximately 45,000 Canadian military personnel were killed
- Over 100,000 Allied bombers were killed while flying missions
- 6 to 8 million Germans died: 5.5 million of them were soldiers
- Austria lost 384,000 people: 261,000 soldiers, 123,700 civilians
- 4/5 of all Axis soldiers killed, died on the Russian front
- Number of tanks & vehicles: Allies 4,358,649 vs. Axis 670,258
- Number of Artillery & Mortars: Allies 6,792,696 vs. Axis 1,363,491
- Number of ships: Allies 54,931 vs. Axis 1,670
- Barrels of oil: Allies 1,043,000,000 vs. Axis 66,000,000
- Total cost of WW II adjusted to today's dollar: $4.69 Trillion USD
- Allied forces dropped 2.7 million tons of bombs on Europe, mostly on Germany
- Every major German city was bombed to rubble: 15 of them were also firebombed with temperatures reaching as high as 1400°F
- Approximately 3.6 million homes in Europe were destroyed leaving over 7.5 million Europeans homeless
- Just over 500,000 German soldiers were captured by the Russians. They stayed in forced labor camps until 1956, when the West German and Austrian governments were finally able to negotiate their release. By then only about 5,000 were still alive. The rest had all been worked to death.

* By comparison 20 million people died in World War I: 10 million military and 10 million civilians

Contents

Foreward	11
1. A Promising Start	17
Our Family Before the War	24
2. The National Socialists	28
3. Joining the Wehrmacht	39
Our Family During the War	47
4. Fate Intervenes	50
5. Journey into Harm's Way	65
My Parents	72
6. The War Arrives	74
7. Flight from Linz	87
8. The SS Death Pact	96
9. Exodus	108
10. Safe Surrender	117
11. Aftermath	123
12. The Russian Occupation	131
Elfi and Me	143
13. Oh Canada!	144
Our Family After the War	148
14. Post Script	156
15. Personal Reflections	159
Author Bio	164
Sources	165
Modern Day Linz, Austria	169

Foreward

Heinrich Dolezal

Throughout my childhood, this picture of my father sat on the fireplace mantel of our Toronto home. In the photo, he is young and handsome in his smart, new uniform. I never gave the picture a second thought until a classmate came to visit. As we passed through the living room she stopped to stare at it. Then she shot me a startled look and asked: *"Was your father a Nazi?"*

I'm not going to pretend that I remember what I said back to her: I was, after all, only about ten. I do however, remember what she said next: *"My father fought the Nazis. He was almost killed!"*

As soon as she said that, a wave of shame washed over me. I'd heard about the Nazis and knew that they'd done awful things, but hadn't connected their actions to my father. For the first time in my life I wondered if my beloved papa was secretly a horrible person.

The episode passed, but the doubts lingered. From time to time I found myself wondering if my father had ever done anything to deserve my shame or if he'd ever killed anyone. I buried those concerns because I loved him very much. He was calm and kind, and always either at work or fixing things around the house. I never once heard him raise his voice, let alone raise a hand against anyone. Still, questions remained. I knew that one day I would have to find out what part he played in the war.

That time came when I was in university. A third-year course on 20th century European history finally got me to act. I bought a notebook and began interviewing my father starting with his childhood. What emerged was a stunning saga of hardship and harrowing close calls, of personal bravery and heartbreaking loss. I was shocked to learn that he once even stood face-to-face with Adolph Hitler.

I never heard him talk about his wartime experiences to anyone else. He was that kind of person - quiet and private. I'm certain that he wouldn't have told me his story if I hadn't pulled it out of him. When I asked him about that, he simply said that he didn't want to burden anyone with his troubles.

Even though a great deal of time has past since World War II, this is a story that the descendants of Heinrich Dolezal need to know. Actually, it's a story that we all need to understand given history's awful habit of repeating its worst chapters.

Ingrid Dolezal Bens

*Accurate scholarship can
Unearth the whole offence
From Luther until now
That has driven a culture mad,
Find what occurred at Linz
What huge imago made
A psychopathic god...*

*W.H. .Auden.
September 1. 1939*

Chapter 1
A Promising Start

My father, Heinrich Dolezal, was born in the small industrial city of Linz, Austria on October 30, 1918. Adolph Hitler had been born in a nearby village in 1889, just before his family moved to Linz. Both men spent their early years in roughly the same neighborhood. Both men's families were laid to rest in the same small cemetery in the Linz suburb of Leonding.

Adolph's father, Alois worked for the civil service as a custom's official. This gave the Hitler family a secure but rather modest income. By comparison, my father's family was far more prosperous. That's because my grandfather, Heinrich Dolezal Sr, was a pharmacist who owned a busy downtown apothecary. While they were young, my father and his older brother Walter enjoyed a comfortable life that included frequent family vacations.

Heinrich and Walter also had a prominent grandfather. Joseph Dolezal was a magistrate in the nearby city of Krems, which lies just east of Linz along the north shore of the Danube. The judge was a stern and distant man who was never seen wearing anything but a three-piece suit. My father's only recollection of his grandfather was that he and his brother had to kneel to kiss his ring whenever they went to visit.

In addition to his son, the judge had three daughters: Barbara, Hermine and Helene. He must have been a relatively enlightened parent since he made sure that his three girls were well educated. Two of them eventually became teachers. To secure his only son's future, the judge sent him to study pharmacy at the University of Krems, which remains a respected technical institute to this day.

From all accounts, my grandfather, Heinrich Dolezal senior, was a very intelligent and highly articulate man. He met my grandmother, the beautiful Elisabeth Weissenhofer, at a chamber music concert shortly after he moved to Linz. They had an immediate connection and were soon married. Elisabeth was from a cultured family with a long Austrian lineage. Although she didn't receive any formal education beyond grade eight, she did attend an excellent finishing school where she perfected her domestic and social skills.

Henrich senior and Elisabeth must have made a striking couple as they walked around Linz. He was extremely tall, with a head of red hair and an impressive handlebar moustache. She was a natural beauty who always dressed well. I remember seeing a picture of my grandmother when she was around twenty, wearing a beautifully tailored suit that featured a pair of fox pelts at the collar: the height of fashion in its day.

Because my grandfather had a successful business, he and his bride were able to rent a spacious apartment. This apartment was in an imposing four-story building, located on Bethlehemstrasse (Bethlehem Street), not far from downtown. Their building had a large cobblestone courtyard that was surrounded by tall iron gates. Inside there were sweeping circular staircases with elaborate wrought iron railings. The building's apartments featured generous rooms with large windows. My grandmother must have been very pleased to be starting married life in such comfortable surroundings.

The young couple soon welcomed two healthy boys, born within a year of each other. Their first son, Walter was a beautiful blond baby. Their second son, Heinrich was a brunette. From the very start, the brothers were close and did everything together. They were also both studious and showed great promise.

While Linz always comes up short when compared to either Vienna or the more scenic Salzburg, it's not without its charms. The city has long been a prosperous industrial hub. That affluence enabled the citizens to construct a number of major religious and cultural centers. Over the centuries many four and five-story buildings with ornate Renaissance and Baroque facades had been erected. These added a prosperous air to the city. Linz also has parks both inside the city and along the Danube. Across the river from downtown there's a small mountain named Pöstlingberg, which is popular for day trips. A young Adolph Hitler is said to have liked to go to the top of that hill to take in the views of the city and dream of greatness. Just beyond the city's limits lie vineyards that have been producing wine since Roman times.

In the early days of their marriage, life in Linz was good for my grandparents and their two sons. The apothecary was doing well and the boys were healthy and bright. What Elisabeth didn't fully comprehend for almost a decade was that her husband was a hopeless alcoholic. She eventually came to learn that he was also a pathological liar. These two failings worked together something like this:

He would open the apothecary in the morning, then close right after lunch so that he could sneak off to one of the many local taverns. There he would drink copious amounts of both beer and alcohol. At some point he would seek out the proprietor. In those days, beer gardens produced their own sausage, so he would set about to convince the various tavern owners that he could provide them with the spices they needed, at rock-bottom prices. Tavern owners looking to improve their profit margins would make a verbal agreement and invariably would not charge him for his drinking spree.

Unfortunately, he never delivered the promised goods. As a result of his subterfuge, he constantly had to find new tavern owners to swindle. This quest took him ever further from downtown on the local trams. He managed to hide his scam for a while, but eventually began to stagger home ever later into the evening. In addition to cheating local tavern owners, it soon came to light that he'd also been drinking away all of the income that his pharmacy produced.

Over time Elisabeth had gradually became aware of her husband's heavy drinking, especially since he was increasingly short of money. To make up for the shortfall, my grandmother began a small sewing business which she operated from their apartment. It wasn't long before the tiny amount she earned was all the family had to buy food.

In addition to cheating tavern owners, my grandfather had also been failing to pay for the ingredients needed to compound drugs. Soon chemical companies stopped supplying him. As money became tighter, Heinrich senior began to steal the money his wife earned from her tailoring business. Before long the family could barely afford to eat.

This financial disaster climaxed on a dark and frigid Sunday in January of 1932. Heinrich and Walter were playing cards on the floor of their room when their father appeared in the doorway. The look on his face made it clear that he was in a sour mood. He ordered my father to go to the pharmacy with a list of compounds to fetch. He sent my father, because it was his younger son who always helped him unpack shipments. My father was a born organizer who had learned to efficiently repackage and label compounds. Heinrich senior knew that young Heinrich would know where to find the things he needed.

My father trekked through the frost-covered streets, found the drugs on the list and brought them to his father, who immediately took them to his bedroom. Then there was silence: hours of it. The boys did homework and read quietly, while their mother cooked and sewed. No one said a word. Just before dinner Elisabeth opened the door to their bedroom. To her horror she saw her husband lying dead in their bed. He had used the chemicals he'd asked his son to fetch, to commit suicide. He knew that his business was about to collapse and had decided to escape the catastrophe that was about to descend upon his family. He did this without saying a word of goodbye to his wife or to his two young sons.

There was of course, the initial shock of having a dead body in the house. Elisabeth immediately sent the boys to stay with a neighbor. There wasn't much sadness though. Heinrich senior had been a thoughtless husband and an indifferent father. He'd never beaten them, but he'd been harming them in other ways for years. Heinrich Dolezal senior was 43 when he died, Elisabeth was 32, Walter was 15 and my father was 14.

In the aftermath of her husband's death, my grandmother found out just how indebted he'd become. Not only was she unable to get anything from the sale of the pharmacy business, she soon discovered that she actually owed a small fortune. For weeks suppliers came to the apothecary to take back their stock. Whatever little she earned from the sale of various store fixtures, immediately went to repay suppliers and months of unpaid rent at both the shop and at home. At the same time as the Dolezal family was struggling under the weight of their personal financial calamity, the world around them was plunging ever deeper into a profound economic depression. It was 1932 and the economy was collapsing.

Given all of this, it would be natural to assume that things got worse for the family, but my father said that life actually improved after his father's death. That's because Elisabeth was an extremely talented seamstress in an era when urban women wore tailored suits. Soon a steady stream of ladies was coming and going from the apartment. Even in the midst of a terrible depression, she was able to expand her business, largely because she charged less than established tailors.

To help out, her sons took part-time jobs. Heinrich and Walter made deliveries for local shops, where they also helped to keep the shelves stocked. Although it took many, many months, Elisabeth eventually paid off the oppressive debt. Without an alcoholic husband stealing from her, the family finally had enough to eat. My father recalled that his mother made new suits for Walter and him as soon as the debts were paid. They were the only new clothes they'd had in years. He said that the first time he and his brother put on their new outfits, the three of them cried.

The tears are understandable. Their situation had been so dire and the three of them had been struggling for so long, that they hadn't allowed themselves to feel anything. Finally, all that bottled-up anguish poured out. This is a sad state of affairs that can only be fully comprehended by those who've had to endure an alcoholic parent. With the trauma of Heinrich senior's death finally behind them, the Dolezal family moved forward. For the next few years things were calm at home. Finances became more secure and the boys did well at school. Unfortunately, a cataclysm of epic proportions was about to descend upon them with full fury.

Our Family Before the War

Elizabeth's Engagement Photo

Joseph Dolezal, Magistrate of Krems

Heinrich Sr and Elizabeth's Wedding Portrait

Heinrich 2, Elizabeth, and Walter 4

Grandma Piribauer's Engagement Photo

Chapter 2
The National Socialists

In 1933 Adolph Hitler became the duly elected leader of Germany. As soon as he gained power, the Nazi movement shifted into high gear. Hitler's speeches were now constantly on the radio. Movie theaters featured newsreels showing massive rallies of ecstatic followers. Hitler was shown touring factories that were once again operating at full capacity. People talked excitedly about restoring pride and prosperity. It was a kind of *Make Germany Great Again* sentiment that was eagerly received by both Germans and Austrians worn down by decades of war and economic hardship.

Both Germany and Austria had come out of World War I in terrible condition. The Allies had severely punished them when they lost the dreadful war that they'd jointly started. In the spirit of retribution, the victors imposed steep reparations and stripped away a number of valuable territories. Germans and Austrians were humiliated and outraged by these punishments. That anger became the fertile ground into which Adolph Hitler sowed the seeds of discontent.

Despite massive displays of fervor, not everyone was happy about the rise of the National Socialists. In fact, a significant number of people spoke out when they first came to power. One German protest group, the well-organized *White Rose* movement, was very vocal. They staged protests, circulated negative flyers about the new regime and painted anti-Nazi graffiti onto buildings. In order to quash them, and all other opponents, the Nazis began to exterminate their critics almost as soon as Hitler became German Chancellor. The newly formed SS corps, in cooperation with local police forces, hastily set up a chain of small internment camps. Within months of Hitler's ascent, these camps began to handle the many Germans who dared disapprove of the regime.

A single government executioner, named Johan Reichart, was hired to travel from site to site with a portable guillotine in the back of his truck. He alone is said to have killed three thousand Germans. Many thousands more were hanged or shot. In all, it's estimated that more than 77,000 German citizens were executed in the early days of Hitler's regime, many of them elected officials. At first, the Nazis tried to keep the mass killing of their own people quiet, but once they'd successfully consolidated their grip on power, they no longer minded if people knew that opposition of any sort would result in death.

Inside Austria a number of national politicians warned against being drawn into German politics. They reminded the public about what had happened when they'd joined forces with the German Kaiser to take part in the disaster that was World War I: Austria had lost its empire. Unfortunately, these warnings went unheeded. The overwhelming number of Austrians were energized by the prospect of economic and social revival. As

Nazi zeal increased, local chapters sprang up everywhere. In Linz, enthusiastic nationalists put up banners, organized rallies and held parades. Soon, local newspapers were extolling the virtues of the Third Reich. Adolph Hitler was from Linz after all!

Ever since the Middle Ages, Austrians had been greeting each other with the phrase *Gruss Gott,* which literally translates as *Greet God.* This was testament to the fact that Austria had been a solidly Catholic country for centuries. Without warning or consultation, the Nazi party let it be known that people should henceforth greet each other by saying *Heil Hitler.* Soon the old familiar God was no longer mentioned; instead Hitler's name was on everyone's lips. The effect of hearing his name everywhere, all day long, reinforced Hitler's status as the new national savior.

The Nazi propaganda machine was also very good at manipulating public opinion through film. One day Walter and Heinrich went to a matinee. Before the feature film a short newsreel showed well-armed Polish forces attempting to over-run a radio station in a small German border town. The boys watched in horror, not realizing that it was a total fabrication. There was no Polish army mobilizing to attack Germany. The newsreel had been staged. That and other films were part of an endless stream of fake news designed to make the population feel threatened.

Soon the brothers were seeing newsreels about the evils of specific minorities. Gypsies and ethnic groups like the Slavs, were depicted as inferior peoples who were diluting the purity of the Aryan race. Other films featured scientist presenting "proof" that disabled people, homosexuals and those suffering from mental illness were also a threat to the German gene pool. The majority of the fearmongering newsreels however, focused on the Jews, who were portrayed as greedy hoarders of cash who were stealing from decent, hardworking Germans. Before long, the desired effect took hold. People could be overheard in the streets and in the shops, talking about the urgent need to take strong action against the many enemies of the glorious new Reich: enemies that didn't actually exist.

Despite the political and economic turmoil roiling the country, the Dolezal brothers made excellent progress. In 1933 Walter finished elementary school with high marks and entered an academic high school. When my father completed grade eight the following year, he enrolled in trade school instead. Acquiring a trade is a time-honored European tradition: besides Heinrich had always been extremely good with his hands. Since Linz was the steel city of Austria he figured that it would be easy to find a good-paying job working with metal. It would turn out to be the most fateful decision of his life. By the spring of 1938 my father had completed both his studies and his apprenticeship. At the age of twenty Heinrich Dolezal had become a master metalsmith. He had demonstrated that he could work in any medium from tin and copper to steel.

Before he could receive his professional certification Heinrich was required to design and fabricate a functional object made entirely of metal. He decided to make a steel vase. This vase was very complex: it narrowed above the base, in the middle and again at the top. At first glance it looked as if it had been made by soldering forty separate pieces together. The amazing thing about the vase was that my father constructed it from a single continuous sheet of steel, as if it were a work of metal origami. When finished, the vase was perfectly symmetrical and without visible seams. Heinrich's instructor was so impressed with his craftsmanship that he urged him to enter his masterpiece in Austria's annual industrial arts competition. Despite there being dozens of entries in the metalsmithing category, my father's vase won third place. He was told to be present at the awards ceremonies to be held in April of 1938.

Heinrich Dolezal was completing his studies just as Austria was being annexed into the Third Reich. On March 11, 1938, the Nazis suddenly announced that Austria would henceforth be part of Germany. After years of non-stop propaganda, there was no resistance. In fact, the citizens of Linz gave German troops an enthusiastic welcome when they marched into the city one day later. Nazi banners adorned every building and happy crowds jammed the streets. Their native son was returning in triumph!

Hitler arrived in Linz during the afternoon of March 12th. By chance, my father found himself swept up in the jubilant crowd that was going to hear him speak in the main square. A few minutes later his Aunt Helene tapped him on the shoulder. She'd recently moved to Linz to teach mathematics at a local grammar school. She suggested they go to hear the speech together.

Heinrich's Aunt Helene was a flamboyant character. She was a tall redhead who wore brightly colored clothing while everyone else was wearing gray. She was also a highly intelligent free thinker. If anyone in the family was capable of understanding what the Nazi were up to, it was Aunt Helene.

Heinrich and his Aunt found a spot fairly close to the balcony from which Hitler addressed the jubilant crowd. It seems that the speech didn't make much of an impression on my father, who remembered almost nothing that the Reich's Fuhrer said. Aunt Helene however, understood it all too well. As they walked away she told her nephew that she found Hitler's remarks to be extremely frightening. Once they were out of earshot of the crowd she turned to my father and said, *"Hitler is going to get us all killed."*

Heinrich was surprised by his Aunt's grim assessment. He had a hard time believing that so many people could be so completely wrong. Everyone in both Austria and Germany seemed ecstatic about the rise of the Third Reich. Because of that fervor, he assumed that his Aunt must be mistaken. He pushed her warning to the back of his mind.

What Hitler said from that balcony in Linz's main square was that the annexation of Austria had a deeper meaning. He proclaimed: *"If Providence once called me forth from this town to be leader of the Reich, it must in doing so have charged me with a mission and that mission could only be to restore my dear homeland to the German Reich."* The citizens of Linz cheered this wildly, ignoring the fact that he'd started his speech by calling them Germans and that he had falsely implied that Austria had ever been part of the modern German state.

To make the takeover complete, the Nazis changed the name of Austria. It was announced that it would henceforth be known as the German province of Ostmark. The Austrian people were never consulted about the name change. Overnight they'd been robbed of their historic identity. Austria was now part of the fatherland, even though the Austrian people are about as similar to Germans as the Scots are to the Irish, or the Australians are to the Canadians. Both nations spoke the same language, but Austria had had its own identity for centuries. For generations it had been the largest empire in Europe. Overnight Austria became just another cog in the Nazi war machine.

Hitler only stayed in Linz for a few hours that day. After his speech in the main square, he left for Vienna where he spoke to an even larger crowd of delirious followers. A few weeks later however, he returned to his hometown for a more leisurely visit. This time a huge parade was held and Hitler attended a number of presentations and special events. Among the planned events was my father's industrial arts awards ceremony.

As soon as the itinerary was published in the Linz newspaper, Heinrich's fellow apprentices began slapping him on the back and telling him how lucky he was to be meeting the great man. I asked my father if he had indeed felt lucky. He said that he'd been quite thrilled at first, but that those positive feelings evaporated the moment he stood face-to-face with the Fuhrer.

The ceremony for the industrial arts winners was held in a large gymnasium. Winning entries, in a range of categories from metal work to innovative engine design, were displayed on tables scattered around the room. Prize winners were told to stand beside their creations to wait for the Reich's Chancellor to approach.

When Hitler got to my father's table, he walked straight up to him, looked deep into his eyes and proceeded to stare in silence. After what seemed like an eternity, Hitler suddenly stepped back and flipped Heinrich his small indoor salute; the one with the bent elbow. Not knowing what else to do, my father saluted back. Then Hitler handed him a signed copy of his book, *Mein Kampf,* (*My Struggle*) which attendants were carting around behind him. Hitler didn't say a word. He didn't take an interest in any of the winning pieces or congratulate anyone on their achievement. There was no friendly banter. All of his interactions were silent, perfunctory and cold.

I asked my father what it felt like to be that close to one of the most diabolical human beings to have ever lived. He said that the encounter had had a very sinister feel to it. Apparently he wasn't the only one who felt the darkness. Before Hitler had arrived the place had been abuzz with anticipation. As the Fuhrer moved about the room, everyone fell silent. By the time he left, the atmosphere had become somber. No one chatted and no one smiled. Those sinister feelings foreshadowed what was about to happen to them, to their families and to their city.

When Adolph Hitler came to power in 1933, he'd been penniless. As soon as he became Chancellor of Germany, he ordered the government to print and pay for, hundreds of thousands of copies of his unreadable tome, *Mein Kampf.* These books were sent to shops in every corner of Germany and Austria, and it soon became a best seller. Hitler pocketed the proceeds from these sales and became an instant millionaire.

The copies of *Mein Kampf* for sale in stores were cheap, hardcover versions. The one Adolph Hitler handed my father was a signed, limited edition copy bound in goose leather of all things. These special-edition versions were selectively given out by Hitler himself and only to people who'd provided distinguished service to the Reich. It's a mystery why a lowly group of students would be given a signed, limited-edition copy of *Mein Kampf* since such copies were typically reserved for Hitler's inner circle. My father's guess was that he was showing off to the hometown crowd.

When Heinrich took his exclusive copy of *Mein Kampf* to school the next day his fellow apprentices were awestruck. The headmaster personally escorted him around to every workshop so that he could hold up his book and tell of his experience. They especially wanted to see the signature of the great man. *"What was it like to meet him?"* they asked. My father said that it had been thrilling and left it at that. He didn't tell them how dark and depressing it had actually been.

Right after the annexation of Austria, life in Linz was good. The economy had picked up considerably during the early years of the Nazi regime, which meant that people were feeling prosperous and hence, more positive. Against that backdrop, the population decided to ignore the disturbing hate speech coming out of the Nazi party. They also didn't appear to be distressed by the fact that the local chapter of the party had erected bulletin boards all over town that were full of damning indictments against the Jews.

As time went on rumors began to circulate that many prominent Jewish families had left the country. An estimated 100,000 Austrian Jews saw the writing on the wall and fled quickly. Unfortunately, another 100,000 stayed. They probably thought that if they kept a low profile nothing too bad would happen to them. They had no idea of the depth of depravity and outright evil at the heart of Nazism. By the end of the war, over 65,000 of the Austrian Jews who made the terrible mistake of staying, had been killed.

Within weeks of my father's encounter with Herr Hitler, the Austrian Nazi Party took control of the city. It was the moment they'd been waiting for. Without warning or due process, Linz city officials including the mayor, the chief financial officer and the head of the local radio station were taken out and shot: their bodies tossed into hastily dug pits. Within days, the Gutenberg Printing Company was taken over and began to publish *Der Arbeitersturm (The Worker's Storm)* which was nothing more than a hate rag.

At about that same time, the Jewish owners of Linz's largest department store, Kraus & Shieles, were arrested. The men were sent to Dachau. The women and children were sent to an as yet unnamed extermination center. Their home was occupied. Their Klimpts and other artworks were taken from their walls and crated up. A sign was posted in their store's window that read, *"Open for Business and Under New Management."* The good citizens of Linz saw this and looked the other way. Perhaps they'd bought the lie that getting rid of the Jews was for the best. Or maybe they'd already figured out that it could be deadly to object.

The great roar of the crowd attending Hitler's first speech in Linz on March 12th, had carried across the Danube to the apartment where the Jewish brothers, Alexander and Eduard Spits, lived above their wine shop. Their family had owned the shop for generations. They must have known what the roar of the crowd meant. They'd heard about the camps and thought that being sent there would be worse than death. A week after the speech that my father and his Aunt heard, the Spitz brothers hanged themselves.

These horrendous acts caused barely a ripple in the city since the government, the police and all of the media were now firmly under Nazi control. Within weeks of the takeover of Austria, there was literally no one left alive who was capable of mounting any sort of protest. People surely heard rumors about the Nazi's reign of terror against their own people, but no one said anything. The citizens of Linz put their heads down and got on with their daily lives.

Chapter 3
Joining the Wehrmacht

A few months after Hitler's April visit to Linz, my father and his brother were conscripted: Walter was 21 and Heinrich was 20. When they received their uniforms, they were told to wear them proudly around town. So, the two handsome brothers walked around in their smart new outfits. Everywhere they went, people stopped what they were doing to clap and cheer. That's when that picture of my father was taken, down on the south bank of the Danube.

Before long the brothers were sent to basic training. They were to be part of the army or *Wehrmacht*. It was September of 1938 and the Nazis were mobilizing for the invasions of Czechoslovakia and the eastern half of Poland. These takeovers were part of their goal to make Germany the largest nation in Europe. Of course, the young people being conscripted were told a very different story. The Nazis convinced them that Germany was under threat of invasion and that they were needed to defend the homeland. They were also told that it was their duty to reclaim the lands that had been unjustly stolen from them after the last war.

When I asked my father what it was like being in Hitler's army, he said that it had been fun at first. Young people who had only ever lived with their parents, finally got to be away from home. The boot camp he and Walter attended was situated in a beautiful forested area just west of Vienna. There they learned to shoot and fight in various terrains. They also learned how to read maps, navigate with a compass and drive a variety of vehicles. Every day began with either a film clip or briefing about the great work of the Fuhrer and the glorious destiny of the Third Reich. Everyone was very enthused!

In their off hours the recruits went swimming in a nearby stream and paraded through local villages in their smart new uniforms. Everywhere they went the locals treated them like heroes, cheering as they passed. They were having a great time. Sadly, the carefree months spent at the training camp would be the last fun these young people would have before virtually all of them were killed. Why did so many Austrians perish in the war? Because they were disproportionately sent to fight on the horrendous Russian front, from which almost no one returned.

From time to time the recruits were sent to repair a road or reinforce a bridge. It was during one of those work assignments that Heinrich got his first glimpse into the inner ugliness of the Reich. Working along-side the recruits on a project to rebuild a bridge, were several prisoners. They didn't appear to be German or Austrian since the guards were shouting at them in some other language. A few looked somewhat swarthy, as if they might have been gypsies. Their prison garb was filthy and they were bone thin. Several looked to be on the verge of collapsing.

When one of the emaciated prisoners suddenly sat down, a guard rushed over and began to batter him with the butt of his rifle. When the exhausted man failed to get up, the guard kicked him in the stomach. This caused the poor man to topple over. The guard then started to savagely kick him in the head. Blood splattered in all directions as the guard continued to kick the man's face. He didn't stop until it was quite obvious that the poor wretch was dead. A few minutes later the body was dragged away and casually flung into a ditch.

As he watched the man being murdered before his eyes, a feeling of total horror swept over Heinrich. He had never seen such brutality! Neither had any of the other recruits. My father said that all of them were stunned into silence. Since armed guards were watching every move, no one said a word. Somehow it was understood that anyone who spoke out could very well meet the same end. When the recruits got back into their vehicle at the end of the day, no one spoke or made eye contact.

Despite how he felt, my father told me that he somehow knew that the horrendous incident could not be discussed, not even with his fellow soldiers. After just a short time in the army he'd already figured out that it was impossible to know what you could say or to whom you could say it. All of the instructors at the camp were fanatical Nazis and his fellow recruits seemed totally enthralled with Hitler. The only thing he ever heard from any of them was that the glorious Reich was their destiny. He never heard so much as a whisper of criticism. As he had done after meeting the Fuhrer, Heinrich buried his doubts. A few days later, they shipped out.

The young men had been at the training camp for about four months when they were deployed. Although Walter had been housed in a different building throughout basic training, the brothers had been able to see each other almost every day. Sadly, on the morning they shipped out, they weren't able to say goodbye. As he watched Walter disappear into the back of a truck, Heinrich suddenly realized that he didn't know if he would ever see him again. It was a crushing blow. They'd always done everything together. Now they were being wrenched apart. For the entire duration of the war Heinrich and his mother wouldn't know where Walter was or even if he was still alive.

The trucks set off without the recruits being told where they were going. That was standard practice for the Nazis. Keeping everybody in the dark was a reminder to the young men that they were no longer in control of their lives. After about an hour's drive my father's group reached a small airfield just south of Vienna. World War II was still far off when my father arrived at his first base.

That's when Heinrich Dolezal got super lucky. He was singled out because of his metalsmith credentials. The little airfield needed lots of improvements before it could properly service the *Luftwaffe (Air Force)*. My father was perfectly suited for the challenge. It turns out that Heinrich possessed a rare skill. He not only knew how to use tools, he even knew how to forge them. He had acquired that ability because he was left-handed. Since most metal-working tools were made for right-handed people, he had learned to make his own tools early on.

Soon he was building the specialized benches needed to bend metal and forging the tools needed to undertake repairs at the airfield. While he did take part in some additional training, most days he was building partitions inside the administrative buildings, fashioning railings for walkways and putting up gutters. He was in and out of every building and everyone knew him.

From time to time Heinrich was required to stand guard. It was during an early morning stint at the main gate that he met my mother. Theresa Piribauer, known to her friends as Resi, was a shy young girl who worked in the kitchen. Civilian workers lived off the base and were allowed to come and go freely. Her home village of Breitenau was only about 20 kilometers from the base. For her, the job represented liberation. There was no work in her little hamlet, so she was very excited to be earning her own money. She was 17 years old.

It was a first love for both of them and they fell for each other quickly. When I pressed my father for information about their romance, he admitted that they didn't have much of one. Apparently they did what other couples confined to a military base did: they sat around and had drinks with their friends and occasionally managed some time alone. Since the hamlet of Breitenau was nearby, Heinrich periodically accompanied his new girlfriend home to meet her family.

My mother was the twelfth and last child, of a large farm family. There were seven boys and five girls. Her father Joseph didn't own the land he farmed, but was merely a tenant on a large estate. Like most tenant farmers, the Piribauer family was dirt poor. Their tiny row house in the village, consisted of just two rooms. Throughout my mother's childhood they had neither electricity nor running water. The only thing they had in abundance was love. Their mother Berta was a kind and caring woman who somehow managed to feed her large brood. Their father Joseph was a hard-working man who toiled outdoors in all kinds of weather and subsequently felt entitled to drink at the local tavern at the end of every day. He was not an alcoholic, but he did manage to drink away a considerable amount of the money that should have gone to feed his large brood. Despite their poverty, my mother's family was a warm and happy one.

By the time Heinrich visited my mother's family, three of her sisters had married and moved to homes of their own. All of her brothers were gone too. They'd been sent to the eastern front. Resi's mother showed my father their letters, which were filled with optimism for a speedy victory and an imminent return home. The brothers' optimism was somewhat warranted at that stage of the war. In September of 1939 the Nazis quickly conquered the western half of Poland. The superior German forces with their high-speed Panzers easily crushed the antiquated Polish military, a portion of which was still fighting on horseback.

If the Nazis had been satisfied with the conquest of the western half of Poland, the expansion of the German Reich would have been accomplished almost overnight. If they'd simply consolidated their early gains they would have succeeded in achieving their goal of creating the largest nation in Europe. But then they let their arrogance cloud their judgment. Instead of stopping after the easy takeover of Austria, most of Czechoslovakia and the western half of Poland, they made the fatal mistake of invading Russia. Hitler and the Nazis were feeling invincible.

At the time my father was reading the letters that Resi's brothers had written, no one in Austria could have imagined that the powerful Nazi war machine would suffer one setback after another. Nor could they have imagined that millions of soldiers who fought on the side of Germany would soon be gone: shot, starved or frozen to death inside Russia. When the war ended, only one of Resi's seven brothers would still be alive. Franz somehow made his way back to his mother. Her six other brothers all died in the nightmare that was the eastern front: gone without a trace!

Since a catastrophe of that magnitude was unimaginable during those early days of the war, my parents didn't realize that they were in the proverbial calm before the storm. In fact, they were feeling fortunate to have met since they would never have found each other if it hadn't been for the war. They were certainly right about that, given that they were from such different backgrounds. He was raised in the city, while she'd grown up in a rural village. He was quiet and reserved, while she was bubbly and outgoing. His Czech/Austrian background gave him a tall, slim frame, high cheekbones and straight brown hair. Her Romanian genes gave her curly black hair, an olive complexion and a short, curvy figure. It was a classic case of opposites attracting.

Although they worked in different parts of the airfield, my parents managed to see each other almost every day. Throughout the remainder of 1939 and the first part of 1940, life at the base was tranquil. During that brief period of calm my parents became deeply committed to each other. Occasionally they even managed to sneak away on their own. A favorite hangout was a small cave in the woods just a short walk from the airfield. Groups of soldiers went there at night to drink by a campfire and have a bit of fun. My father says that he and my mother really enjoyed those quiet months. That time was a blessing because the years that followed would bring them nothing but trauma and loss. By the spring of 1942 their brief period of peace was over. The ground war was heating up and the Reich needed more men at the front.

Our Family During the War

My Mother's Brothers and Sisters

Walter's Conscription Photo

Theresa's Engagement Photo

Chapter 4
Fate Intervenes

Redeployment was announced and once again few details were provided. Bits of information leaked by the office staff indicated that all of the airfield's recruits were destined for the Russian front. Over the centuries the Russians had earned a formidable reputation because no one had ever been able to conquer them. They were fierce fighters and their winters were deadly. As a result, that front was the one place no one wanted to go.

On the morning he was to ship out, Heinrich got a reprieve that would ultimately save his life and, by extension, the lives of his descendants. He was sitting in his barrack waiting to be loaded into a truck, when someone called his name. He was told to take his gear and report to the office. There he was informed that he would not be going to the dreaded eastern front, but to the recently annexed Czech provinces instead.

Shortly after they took hold of Austria in 1938, the Nazis annexed the two richest provinces of Czechoslovakia. The pretext given was that these regions contained a significant German-speaking population that rightfully belonged inside the Reich. The massive Nazi war machine encountered no armed resistance and quickly overtook the prosperous Czech provinces of Bohemia and Moravia. They renamed the area the Czech Protectorate to give the false impression that they were protecting the people who lived there. What they were actually doing was seizing the Czech people's industrial resources for their war effort.

Although they weren't able to mount any sort of military resistance, the Czechs did protest. Intellectuals in Prague spoke out and students massed in the street. Soon the Nazis were rounding people up. Leading politicians were placed in front of firing squads and shot. Books were burned and protesters were sent to hastily established work camps. Within weeks, staunch Nazis occupied every position of power. By the time my father arrived, the Czech Protectorate had been operating for almost two years. During that time, area administrators had discovered that more personnel were needed, especially skilled mechanics and metal workers.

When he got into the truck headed to Moravia, my father recognized two guys from the metal shop at the airfield: Hans Mueller and Freidrick Ganz. The three of them bonded during the short ride north. The trip to their new base, situated in the lush farmland just southwest of the Czech city of Brno, was quick. It turns out that Heinrich Dolezal spent the entire war moving around in a tiny triangle. It's only 155 km from Linz to Vienna, 135 km from Vienna to Brno and 185 km from Brno back to Linz. The entire round trip can be made in a few hours by car. Being shipped to the Brno area was a bit ironic for my father since that's where his father's family had lived for many generations. It turns out that Dolezal is a fairly common Czech name.

My father's new base was a random collection of about a dozen buildings recently constructed on a parcel of empty farmland. This pastoral setting had open fields, small streams and beautiful forests. There were about two hundred military personnel at the base when my father arrived. In addition to the enlisted folks, there were also a dozen or so Czechs working at the site. Although it wasn't an airfield, runways had been scraped into one of the fields so that planes in need of service could land. Barracks had been built, but it soon became apparent to Heinrich that it wasn't a military base, but more of a service center. Troops did not come and go and there was no further training or talk of deployment. He was told that the role of the base was to fix broken equipment so it could be sent back to the front.

Because he had a unique and needed skill, Heinrich Dolezal became one of the lucky few who never actually fought in the war. Just like the enlisted personnel who managed supply lines or handled communications, he found himself working behind the lines. Although he had a uniform, Heinrich rarely wore it at his new base. Most days he was in overalls, which suited him just fine. The more he thought about the horrors of the Russian front, the more he wanted everyone to forget that he even was a soldier.

At his new home, my father coped with the stress of all the endless war talk by staying busy. As he had done at the airfield, he helped to set up an efficient metal shop. He, Hans and Freidrick soon had a reputation for being able to fix anything. The other indispensable asset at the base was the engine shop next door. The two talented mechanics who worked there, Jonas Eisner and Louis Ryker, seemed able to fix any sort of broken engine from either a truck or airplane. Soon the area behind their combined workshops was jammed with trucks that needed an engine overhauled, trailers with broken axles and small planes riddled with bullet holes. Within weeks of my father's arrival, broken-down vehicles and damaged planes began to flood in from the war zone to the east.

Besides being popular inside the compound, Heinrich was well liked by the farmers who came to the base to sell their meat and produce. Soon he was fixing fenders and trailer hitches for them too. Since Austria was so near, most of them spoke German. In fact, that entire region had once been part of the Austro-Hungarian Empire. The commander of the base was Gerhard Bosch, a genial German who was probably very grateful to have landed in this quiet corner of the war. His approach to leadership was strictly laissez faire. As long as the work was getting done and the area farmers were cooperative, he didn't get in the way. He was okay with his people helping the locals since that seemed to work out for everyone.

At some point my father found out that area farmers needed more stills to make moonshine. The farmers already had stills of course, but they'd come to realize that if they each had an additional still or two, they'd be able to increase their production. With all the soldiers stationed in the area, demand for alcohol had skyrocketed, so young Heinrich got into the still-making business.

Over the months the shop had accumulated piles of metal scraps that included pieces of copper tubing. In his off-hours my father used these leftover bits to build stills. On his days off he packed up the pieces and headed out into the beautiful countryside on his bike. He never wore his Nazi uniform on these outings, only his overalls. After he finished soldering their stills together, the local farmers invariably invited him to share a meal. In time they came to like and trust him. It may have been his mild manner or maybe they liked him because he had a Czech surname. Whatever the reason, these friendships would one day save his life.

The still-making business made my father popular inside the base too. Whenever he delivered one of his stills, the farmers would give him at least one free bottle of their home brew. He gave these to Commander Bosch and the guys at the service center. Soon everyone at the base was in favor of Heinrich's still-building business. Even people he didn't know were smiling and waving at him.

At that point in the war, things were calm inside my father's base because they were far from the fighting. Since the locals were making a killing supplying the Nazis with food and booze, everyone around the base was happy. Because they were flush with cash, Heinrich was able to charge the farmers for his stills. It wasn't a lot of money, but it built up. When he had a decent amount, he went to the post office and sent his mother his salary, plus the money he earned from his side-business. As the war dragged on, that money became her only source of income.

Life was blessedly calm for Heinrich Dolezal for a long time. Since he never heard any accurate reports about how badly it was actually going for the Nazis, he didn't have much to worry about. Of course, he missed his new girlfriend, but at least they were able to correspond by mail. That feeling of calm was shattered in March of 1942, when he received a disturbing letter from his mother.

For as long as the Dolezal family had lived in the building on Bethlehemstrasse, there'd been a Jewish family living there. Abraham Weiss owned a hardware store and scrap yard on the outskirts of Linz. He and his wife Nara had two children: Jacob and Miriam. Although Jacob was much younger than my father, the two of them had often played soccer in the courtyard of their building. Right after Heinrich senior's death, Nara had shared food with them on several occasions. They were good neighbors.

Now Elisabeth was writing that the peace of the building had been shattered a few days earlier by the sound of boots stomping up the stairs to the third floor. This was followed by the banging of doors and shouting. The other residents opened their doors to check on the commotion. To their horror they witnessed the Weiss family being taken into custody. Their immediate neighbor on the third floor was alarmed by what she saw and protested. One of the arresting thugs grabbed the woman by the hair and smashed her head into a wall with such force that she was rendered unconscious.

After being allowed to pack a few essentials, the Weiss family members were escorted down the stairs. My grandmother caught a glimpse of them as they passed her doorway. All four of them were crying and clinging to each other. When the arresting party reached the ground floor the commander of the raid shouted into the stairwell at the top of his lungs: *"Anyone who is objecting can come down and join this group of degenerates as they march to their deaths!"*

Heinrich was horrified. He'd taken the letter to the dining hall so that he could read it during his afternoon break. Now he hurried outside so that no one would see how upset he was. He found an isolated spot and finished reading. His mother reported that there were more frightening developments in Linz. Neighbors had seen people being marched out of town. These people had arrived on a barge and were then made to walk east along the north bank of the Danube. One of Elisabeth's friends told her that the Nazis had established a concentration camp in the hills there. Its name was Mauthaussen

The Mauthaussen camp was located next to a major stone quarry. For months barges filled with prisoners continued to land in Linz. These unfortunate people had been collected from all over the expanded Reich. The reason for the camp? None of Elisabeth's neighbors had any idea. It would only become known after the war was over that the camp had been established next to a stone quarry in order to provide the massive granite blocks needed to construct Hitler's two pet projects. It turns out that he planned to glorify himself by building both an enormous cultural center and a massive mausoleum in Linz. Once his work of creating the vast German Empire was complete, he had plans to both retire and then spend eternity in his hometown.

As soon as he'd finished reading the letter, Heinrich destroyed it so that it wouldn't fall into the hands of the fanatics at the base. He couldn't risk having them learn that his mother had sympathy for the Jews. Views like that could get you killed. As he tore her letter to pieces, the horror of Hitler's plan to create a master race began to sink in. The so-called "undesirables" that Hitler had ranted about for years, were being rounded up and enslaved. Once again he knew that he had to conceal how he felt about what the Nazis were doing.

Throughout the remainder of 1942 and all of 1943, while the war raged all over Europe, things remained tranquil in the southern region of the Czech Protectorate. Despite how peaceful it was for him, my father worried constantly about his brother, who he assumed had been sent to the Russian front. No one he knew ever received a letter from anyone stationed on that front once the fighting intensified. As a result, Heinrich and his mother didn't know if Walter was dead or alive for the entire duration of the war.

This information blackout included the base. The only bits of news ever disseminated by the office were propaganda pieces about how well it was going for the Nazis. Throughout the entire war he never heard a single report of setbacks or casualties; only happy talk. Of course, these reports were complete rubbish. By the middle of 1943 things were already going very badly for the Reich. When the body count was tallied at the end of the war, the world would learn that over three million German and Austrian soldiers had died in the futile attempt to defeat the Russians. With very few exceptions, everyone sent to that front was either killed or taken prisoner.

It wasn't until months after the war finally ended that Heinrich and his mother found out what had actually happened to Walter. As suspected, he had been sent to the eastern front. At first he fought in the ground war to overtake the western half of Poland. That part of the war had been relatively easy to win, but then the Nazis pushed east. At the start of the Russian invasion, the Axis forces were divided into three sections. The northern group headed for Leningrad via the Baltics. The central group aimed for Moscow. The southern group set out in the direction of Ukraine in order to capture oil fields and Black Sea ports. Walter Dolezal was deployed in the northern offensive. There he spent two summers engaging Soviet troops in the heavily forested area near Russia's northern border. In the winter, however, he did something very different.

If you've ever watched the winter Olympics, you will have seen something called the Biathlon. It's a crazy-looking event in which contestants race around on skis, then either stand or lie down in the snow to shoot a rifle. That event is modeled on a highly effective warfare tactic perfected in the Nordic countries. That's what my uncle Walter did for two winters in the far north. The Nazis hadn't started out fighting that way, but the Fins had such success fighting the Russian on skis that they were convinced to adopt that tactic for themselves.

During Walter's first winter on skis, the army kept a close eye on him and his fellow skiers. They were regularly picked up and given time to recover, before being sent back into the cold. During his last winter however, the Nazi war effort fell apart and the trucks no longer showed up. They basically left him out there to die. He kept fighting Russians until he ran out of bullets. Sometimes he found bullets and scraps of food near the bodies of fallen colleagues. He kept fighting and skiing until he'd skied right into Finland.

Of course, he had no idea where he was, nor did he care. He was so emaciated and sick by then that he could no longer stand. A Finnish patrol found him just barely alive. The Finns immediately took him to the hospital and saved his life. It may have been because they'd been fighting the Russians too, or maybe it was because he looked so pathetic. In any event they were kind to him, even going so far as to put him on a train home once the war had finally ended.

After months of malnourishment and exposure to the extreme cold, Walter Dolezal had developed a severe case of hydrocephalus. This is a condition in which fluid collects in the brain, enlarging the head and often causing brain damage. It's caused by an imbalance between how much cerebrospinal fluid is produced and how much is absorbed into the bloodstream. Hydrocephalus is a horrible condition that doesn't go away on its own; it requires medical attention. Without help Walter would certainly have died. The Finnish doctors gave him the treatments he needed even though he wasn't one of their soldiers: a remarkable display of both humanity and civility.

Of course, my father had no idea about the horrendous ordeal his brother was enduring while he was safely tucked away in his quiet corner of the war. While he slept in a warm bed, Walter lay in the snow. While Walter ate scraps of dried food, Heinrich enjoyed three warm meals a day. While Walter dodged bullets and bravely engaged the enemy, Heinrich welded car parts in his metal shop. It was a totally unfair situation in which one brother endured extreme hardship and danger, while the other managed to escape the war altogether. Of course, neither brother knew of the other's circumstances. My father just kept hoping that Walter was all right and that his own peaceful situation would last. Unfortunately, he would soon come into contact with the most horrendous aspect of the Third Reich.

It happened on a day when about thirty soldiers from the base were sent to rebuild a broken-down stretch of train tracks. Mid-afternoon on the third day they were ordered to stop working. At first everyone was puzzled about why work had been halted.

A few minutes later, a bedraggled assortment of people began to shuffle by on the tracks. It was an eerie and silent procession. They were moving very slowly and looked exhausted. How long had they been marching?

By then Heinrich was well aware that so called "inferior peoples" were being rounded up, but he'd never personally witnessed such activities. It's one thing to hear about something and quite another to see it in the flesh. Suddenly, the full horror of the Nazi extermination program was right in front of him. The procession went on for ages and was deeply shocking. Hundreds and hundreds of people shuffled by. At first it was mostly men, but then more and more families came along. Men, women and children clutching their meager possessions in dirty bundles. Most were wearing the yellow Star of David on their coats. At one point my father noticed a young man carrying a small girl. Her ringlets hung down over his shoulder. The man looked as if he was about to collapse.

My father told me that the sight of the young father carrying his little girl brought him to tears. It was just too much to bear. Without warning an armed guard lunged at my father and hit his shoulder with the butt of his rifle. Then he pushed him back and barked a warning: *"Be careful or you'll be marching with them!"* In that split second, my father felt whatever last particle of faith he still had in the Nazi enterprise shatter into a million pieces. The inhuman treatment being inflicted on these people was simply too awful. What frightened him equally was the look on the face of that guard; it was pure hatred. Heinrich had seen that look before. It was the same cold, hard stare he had seen on the faces of too many of the Nazis he'd encountered. It was a look that said: *"If you're not with us, we have no use for you! If you get in the way, we will kill you!"*

My father said that he'd become increasingly offended by the endless stream of hateful propaganda circulating at the base. Seeing the brutality of that forced march gave him his final push over the edge. He knew that these poor people were doomed and it sickened him. As he went back to work, Heinrich recalled his Aunt Helene's warning. He hadn't believed her at the time, but he now realized that she'd been right. Hitler really was going to get them all killed!

The evil of the Nazi enterprise was now crystal clear to my father. He'd realized some time back that he had to be careful about what he said. Now he understood that his life meant nothing to the people in charge: they were beyond all morality. My father told me that he barely slept that night. As he lay in the dark, he had a revelation. He realized that he too was a prisoner of the Reich. At the start of the war he'd assumed that the people most likely to take his life were the much-talked-about external enemies. He now understood that his biggest challenge might well be surviving Hitler's army itself.

Although my father never took active part in the war, he did have a front row seat to the hatred and the evil of the Nazis. They had created a culture based on dehumanizing others. Anyone not actively on board with their psychopathic goals knew that their own lives could very well be in danger.

A few months later my father was stopped at a crossing further along that same rail line. The tracks he and his fellow soldiers had helped to repair were fully operational now. He and Hans were in an old truck on their way to Brno to look for metal at a scrap yard. As they waited with a group of local pedestrians, a train started to slowly roll by. There was one cattle car after another, filled not with livestock, but with people. Human beings were being transported like animals. He could see them through the slats. Arms stuck out here and there. Sometimes a face could be seen searching for a breath of fresh air. As one of the cars rolled slowly by he heard a baby wail. In horror he realized that the Nazis were transporting families with infants!

My father said that both he and Hans gasped when they heard the baby. He glanced at the people standing at the crossing and saw that many of them were crying. Crying not only because it was horrifying, but also because they knew that there was nothing they could do to stop it.

Heinrich later heard that a Jewish concentration camp had been built inside the Czech Protectorate. The farmers seemed to know about the camp, which was named Terezin. When my father probed one of the lieutenants at the base about it, he stated flatly that the Nazis wanted the locals to know about the many camps scattered around the Reich. It was his opinion that knowing about the camps encouraged the locals to toe the line out of fear of being sent away to be worked to death. The blank, hard expression on his face as he made that pronouncement gave my father chills.

What neither my father, nor the rest of the world, would know until after the war was over was the enormous scale of the gulag system being built by the Nazis. Once most adult males had been sent to fight, the German high command ramped up the camp system in order to provide forced labor for the war machine. There were large camps, transfer stations and smaller sub-camps. Most were places where men were sent to be slaves.

Some like Auschwitz, were simply extermination facilities. The people sent to these horrific places were the ones who couldn't provide labor like the mentally challenged, the disabled and Jewish women and children. In total the Nazis built and operated a mind-boggling 44,000 forced labor camps, transfer stations, local jails and ghettos. They even had special camps for boys and girls. The Nazi concentration camp system was the largest network of organized state terror to ever exist. An evil distinction if there ever was one.

Henrich was now certain that he had to keep his thoughts to himself. He told me that he no longer dared to even tell Hans, Friedrick or the two mechanics next door how he really felt, for fear that they might be overheard repeating his views. Fortunately for him, it wasn't hard to stay under the radar since his work kept him busy and far from the action. In time he managed to order a second pair of overalls. That was all he wore now: the dirty ones in the shop and the clean ones when he visited the farmers. His Nazi uniform hung in his locker in pristine condition. The pistol in his holster had only ever been discharged at the firing range at his first base. All six of the bullets assigned to him when he arrived in the Czech Protectorate sat idle in their chambers.

Every couple of months my father managed to secure a pass. Then he would put on his pristine uniform for the short train ride to see his mother. This was a highly unusual circumstance in the middle of a war. Virtually all of the men who'd been conscripted were hundreds of miles away. Their families never received so much as a letter from them, let alone frequent visits. Right up until the last months of the war, Heinrich was able to visit Linz on a regular basis.

That's because Austria wasn't bombed until the middle of 1944. During the first three years of the war the Allies were busy destroying cities and industrial centers inside Germany. As a result, things still looked normal in Austria, at least on the surface. Mail was being delivered and the trains were still running, although rarely on time. By early 1944 most of the skilled railway staff had been sent to fight, leaving elderly folk to run the trains. Old men and women were now running everything, often without any real training. As a result, basic utilities like water and electricity were frequently shut off. Worst of all, there was little or no food to be found. The few grocery stores still open were largely empty since farmers had started to hoard whatever they produced.

When my father arrived home just before the Christmas of 1943 he was grateful to see that the grand old apartment building on Bethlehemstrasse was still as he remembered it. Sadly, his mother was not. Elisabeth Dolezal was a strong and resourceful woman who'd already overcome a lot, but now she was a nervous wreck. She worried constantly about her sons and fretted about the prospect of being bombed. Since she no longer had tailoring work to distract her, worrying had become her main preoccupation. When he saw how frantic his mother had become, Heinrich decided that Resi should come to Linz to stay with her so that she wouldn't be alone.

Chapter 5
Journey into Harm's Way

By the time she received my father's letter, my mother was more than ready for a change of scenery. She'd continued to work at the airfield, but was increasingly concerned that they were about to be bombed. That's because of daily reports that the war was coming closer. The possibility of being bombed made her so anxious that she could barely sleep.

On a cold day in December of 1943 Resi was called to the office. With all of the soldiers at the front, the airfield had begun to hire local farmers to do odd jobs. Recently her father Joseph, had started to do maintenance work there. When she got to the office they informed her that he'd collapsed while working in the hangar. Her father had had a massive heart attack.

My poor mother fainted. When she came to they told her that her father's body had been loaded into the back of a truck. She was directed to the main gate, but no one accompanied her. When she got to the truck she saw her father's body lying in the open truck bed, covered only by a thin sheet. Two soldiers offered to drive her to an intersection about two kilometers from her home. Then they loaded a small handcart into the back of the truck. When they got to that intersection the soldiers unloaded the handcart and placed my grandfather's body into it. Then they drove off, leaving my twenty-year-old mother to take her father's body home in the gathering darkness.

As she pushed her wretched cargo down the deserted road, my mother careened between grief and worry about how her mother and sister were going to react. It would be such a terrible shock. Resi pushed her father's body down the frozen country road by herself for over an hour. When she reached Breitenau, a neighbor saw her and helped her push the cart the rest of the way.

Although Resi had eleven siblings, only herself and her sister Hilda were still living at home. As she'd feared, both her mother and sister became hysterical at the sight of Joseph's frozen body. After a great deal of weeping the women lifted him from the cart and carried him to the kitchen table. He lay there for the next two days while villagers came to pay their respects. On the third day he was buried in the church cemetery.

It had finally all been too much for my mother; she was done with the war! My father's letter included train fare, so she left immediately. To Resi it probably felt like she was leaving the war behind when she boarded that train to Linz. She was certain that she would be much safer living in a large apartment building in the middle of a city. She would soon find out that she was terribly mistaken and that she was actually heading straight into the war.

Just a few weeks after my mother arrived in Linz, the Allies started their systematic bombing of both Linz and Vienna. They would bomb these two cities non-stop throughout most of 1944 and the first four months of 1945. In Linz they started with the steel mills and manufacturing plants. Then they bombed key roads and bridges. In due course they turned their attention to the homes.

My father visited Linz once more before the bombs started to rain down. During that visit Heinrich biked to the countryside to buy food. He made covers for the kitchen windows so that their lights couldn't be seen from outside. He fixed their plumbing and found wood for the fireplace, so that they would have heat when the electricity failed. Then he and my mother went to city hall to get married. At least they tried to get married.

It turns out that the Nazis had a fetish for paperwork: you had to have papers for everything. At Linz city hall, the young couple was informed that they would have to prove that there was no Jewish blood in either of their backgrounds before they could wed. When my father pointed out that his fiancé was unable to return to her village to gather documents, they allowed my mother to sign an affidavit attesting to her ethnic purity. That little bit of laxity underscores just how absurd Hitler's racial purity project actually was.

My father on the other hand, was told that he would have to produce birth certificates for all of his ancestors going back four generations. This was a ridiculous hurdle to impose in the middle of a war. The only thing that made the task at all feasible was the fact that my father's ancestors had all lived either in Linz, in the nearby city of Krems, or in the exact part of the

Czech Protectorate where he was stationed. His mother already had the birth certificates of his Austrian relations, but he would somehow have to get hold of those belonging to his Czech ancestors.

When Heinrich got back to the Protectorate he added this new chore to his list of duties. Luckily base commander Bosch understood bureaucracy. He kindly gave my father free time to gather the certificates he needed from local churches. It took Heinrich months to retrieve the required documents. He told me that he found the whole exercise to be totally ridiculous. All over Europe, people were either being killed or were running for their lives, while he ran around gathering bits of paper.

What made the task so difficult was the fact that most of the rural churches he visited were deserted and locked. Then he had to go from house to house asking if anyone knew where he might find the priest. Once he found the priest he had to wait while the man searched the records and then painstakingly transcribed a copy of the needed birth certificate. This totally absurd project went on for weeks. It did have one significant upside though. It enabled my father to travel further into the Czech countryside on his bike. These trips greatly expanded his knowledge of local roads and shortcuts: knowledge that would one day be invaluable.

Finally, all of the needed papers were in order. During my father's next visit home, he and my mother were married. The officials at Linz city hall congratulated them on being Aryans. Then they proudly handed them a marriage certificate emblazoned with Nazi Swastikas. Ironically a recent genetics test revealed that I'm 1% Ashkenazi Jew. A fitting footnote to Hitler's ludicrous quest.

When my father got back to his Czech base after getting married, he was horrified to learn that all of the remaining servicemen, including Hans and Freidrick, were gone. They'd been sent to the Russian front. My father was grief stricken. The three of them had become like brothers. Their friendship had sustained him during the last three years. Standing in the now deserted metal shop, he broke down thinking about what they would have to endure on that terrible front. Deep down he knew he'd never see them again.

Just one day after Heinrich had gone to Linz, a Nazi convoy had rolled into the base. Names had been read out. His name had been among them, but he'd been absent. An hour later all but a few men were gone. Miraculously, Jonas Eisner and Louis Ryker from the engine shop had been spared. Apparently, Commander Bosch had been able to successfully argue that the base needed mechanics to keep servicing broken-down equipment. My father and the mechanics fell to speculating about how long it would be before a truck came for them too. When my father first arrived at the base there'd been more than two hundred enlisted personnel on site. Now the entire workforce consisted of a handful of local Czech employees and six remaining military staff: my father, the two mechanics, commander Bosch and his two underlings in the office.

By early 1944 the Nazis were losing men at a staggering rate on both the eastern and western fronts. That's why they'd come for Freidrick, Hans and the others; they desperately needed more soldiers. Just a few weeks later Heinrich received a letter from his mother reporting that the Nazis had started to enlist old men and young boys. Even though my father didn't have any accurate information about what was actually happening in the war, he felt certain that these poor people were being sent to their deaths.

What Heinrich didn't know at the time was that the Nazis were not only on the verge of defeat in Russia, but that they were also losing on the western front. That information would have shocked him to the core. He would have been even more alarmed to learn that by the spring of 1944 Allied bombers had reduced every significant German city to rubble. The entire nation was in pieces from top to bottom. It was destruction on a scale that no one could ever have imagined.

Since he was the only one left in the metal shop, my father was now working non-stop. He not only had to fix everything that broke, but had to make most of the parts from scraps. In his last months at the base he recalled cutting up empty oil barrels to patch airplane wings. But would that keep him from being shipped out? He guessed that it would not. He considered going to Bosch to make some sort of deal, but realized that it would be too risky. When push came to shove, amiable Bosch was nonetheless a Nazi. Asking to be spared would be tantamount to treason, so my father kept quiet and prayed that they wouldn't be coming for him any time soon.

In addition to his work inside the base he was still helping the locals repair their equipment. One day he was working with a farmer named Jaroslav Dura to fix his broken well pump. He had done numerous jobs for the Dura family over the years and knew them well. The problem was that there were no parts to be found as supply chains had completely broken down. My father took the broken parts to his shop to serve as models and somehow fabricated new ones. The next day he fixed their pump.

The Dura family was ecstatic. Without well water it would have been a struggle to keep their animals and crops adequately watered. After a celebratory dinner, Jaroslav asked my father to follow him. Inside a small haybarn he lowered a trap door in the ceiling. Hidden behind bales of hay in the barn's crawl space was a wireless radio.

My Parents

Heinrich and Theresa Wedding Portrait

Baby Elfrieda, 1945

Chapter 6
The War Arrives

Heinrich instantly understood what it meant to be shown the radio: it was total trust. If the Nazis at the base learned of it, the entire Dura family would be marched into the woods and shot. The next day their farm would be burned to the ground and their animals confiscated. He turned to Jaroslav and crossed his heart. No words were spoken. It was understood that he would never speak of it. It was then that my father finally learned the truth about the war.

The most shocking news my father received that day was about just how badly the German army was being defeated on all fronts. In addition, he was stunned to learn about the extent to which German cities had been utterly destroyed. Of great significance too, was that fact that the Nazis' entire network of factories had been obliterated. That, as much as anything, meant that their fate was sealed. Without factories there was no possible way for them to ever make a comeback. Of more immediate concern to my father, however, was the fact that the war was coming closer.

In February of 1943 the Germans had finally lost the prolonged and brutal battle of Stalingrad. A series of extreme weather events had first bogged their vehicles in mud, then frozen them in place. After that the Russians cut their supply lines and cornered them inside the city. In time, the remaining German troops began to simultaneously starve and freeze. After months of block-to-block fighting inside the ruined city, the few remaining Nazis surrendered. They did so even though Hitler had ordered them to fight to the death.

As soon as German commanders surrendered, the Russian army began to move west. Throughout the war, the Czech Protectorate had been on the sidelines. Now it was in the direct path of the advancing Soviets. To cap off the bad news, Jaroslav reported that the Russians had announced their intention to take possession of the Baltic states, Poland, Hungary, Romania, Ukraine, Czechoslovakia, Bulgaria, Austria and half of Germany. It was their aim to bring these countries into the Soviet sphere. The only hopeful thing my father heard that day was that American and British forces were attempting to take control of Austria.

Of course, no one at the base said a word about how badly things were going for the *Wehrmacht* or about the advancing Russian army. Gerhard Bosch certainly knew the truth because the base had its own wireless radio, but he wasn't talking, at least not to the underlings. He and his two remaining office staff were still going on and on about the glorious Reich. Out in the countryside though, the Czech people knew the truth. The farmers either had wireless radios or knew someone who did. Late at night they listened to Allied broadcasts about troop movements and the surrender of various segments of the German army.

In addition to radio broadcasts, the Allies had lately started to drop leaflets. A friend had given one to Elisabeth who mailed it to my father. These leaflets informed the citizens that they should not be afraid of American, British or Canadian soldiers. The Allies did this for two reasons. First, they didn't want to encounter resistance among the population since they already had their hands full fighting the Nazis. The second reason was that they wanted Axis solders to know that they would receive fair treatment from them.

The leaflets dropped by the Allies proclaimed that any Nazi who surrendered to Allied forces would immediately be allowed to go home. These leaflets also stated outright that anyone who surrendered to the Russian army was guaranteed be sent to a labor camp to be worked to death. These flyers bore the signature of General Dwight Eisenhower, the Supreme Allied Commander in Europe. The Allies were actively enticing enemy soldiers to defect to them. For my father, that promise, signed by Eisenhower, became his sole hope for survival. Of course, he would first have to find a way to escape the base.

Heinrich continued to keep his head down and focus on his work. His only source of information remained Jaroslav, who came to the base once a week to deliver eggs, milk and produce. Jaroslav always brought along some random piece of broken-down equipment so that he had an excuse to visit the metal shop. That's when he shared the latest updates. As the months passed, the reports of Soviet advances became ever more alarming. Each time they met, Heinrich hoped to hear about where he might be able to surrender. Sadly, Jarosalv was never able to report that the Americans were close enough to be reached on foot.

In March of 1944 there was an appalling development at the base when six young boys arrived. Fritz, Ernst and Wilhelm were fifteen, Wolfgang, Leopold and Dieter were only fourteen. They'd been conscripted but had received no training. The boys didn't even have uniforms. They had been given the flimsy cotton outfits of the Hitler Youth, which was basically like a Boy Scout uniform. They had neither boots nor coats. None of them had ever held a gun or fired a single shot.

Heinrich found their arrival to be deeply disturbing. When his mother reported that young boys were being sent to fight, he'd assumed that they were sending youths who were at least eighteen. These lads were still children. Why were they in the Czech Protectorate? No one would tell him. Bosch just shrugged his shoulders and asked my father to train them. Train them for what? Over time my father pieced it together. Since training camps were closed, youths like these were being sent to the remaining military bases to pick up whatever skills they could acquire. These six boys where at the base because they would soon be sent to fight. Given the age of these children, Heinrich knew that deployment would most certainly be fatal.

The Hitler Youth movement had been founded by Adolph Hitler to engage young people in the war effort. At its height, the movement had almost nine million members. Initially the boys were only supposed to support the troops by doing things like run errands and dig trenches. When the Germans began running out of soldiers however, these young people were sent into battle, often with only a few hours of training. In the last weeks of the war, it was common for children aged twelve to fourteen, to be sent to fight. The youngest Hitler Youth member ever to be captured was only eight years of age.

Heinrich quizzed the boys about their backgrounds. Ernst and Wilhelm came from the same western suburb of Linz. Wolfgang and Fritz came from farms in Styria, which is in southern Austria. Leopold and Dieter hailed from Vienna. While all of the boys were unhappy about being separated from their families, Leo was the most traumatized by the separation. He was the smallest of the boys: a pale blond with a slight frame. During the day he seemed alright, but at night he had terrible nightmares. The boys had been put into Heinrich's barrack since it was otherwise empty. My father soon started to sleep on the cot next to Leo to help keep him calm.

During the day Heinrich kept the boys busy. To make Bosch happy he drilled them out in the yard. He shared the fundamentals of hand-to-hand combat and other skills he'd learned in basic training. Sometimes he led them into the woods and made them find good places to hide. The boys were having fun: to them it felt like a game. To my father it was a catastrophe. He told me that at least once a day he wanted to sit down and cry because he knew that they had absolutely no chance of surviving at the front. Somehow he managed to maintain a brave face when he was with them. If he'd told them the truth about their prospects, they would have panicked. Although he was only twenty-six himself, my father said that the whole situation made him feel old.

What really had Heinrich on edge was the prospect of a truck rolling into the base to collect them. This time there would be no reprieve for him: he would have to go. Every time he heard the crunch of tires out in the yard, his blood ran cold. Every night when the gates were locked, he breathed a sigh of relief: he and the boys had been spared one more day.

For the next several months nothing much changed at the base. Broken-down equipment kept arriving, and my father and the mechanics next door worked non-stop. In fact, more broken-down planes and trucks arrived than at any previous time in the war. Since the Nazis had totally lost the ability to manufacture anything new, they'd been reduced to patching up their damaged vehicles. Luckily the boys were eager to help and were soon working hard in both the engine and metal shops.

Meanwhile in Linz, the situation had become deadly since the Allies were now regularly bombing the city. Their first targets were the industrial areas along the river, but bombs were also aimed elsewhere. Soon anyone who had relatives in the countryside or in a town that wasn't being bombed, packed up and fled. As a result, increasingly desolate Linz found itself draped in the heavy air of impending doom. After a few weeks of listening to the sound of bombs crashing into nearby buildings, Resi found herself overwhelmed with the desire to flee the city.

What made matters worse was the fact that that my father hadn't been allowed to visit in months. In May of 1944, he finally secured a five-day pass to visit Linz. When Bosch handed him his pass he went on and on about the fact that it must not be lost. My father found it strange that he was so worked up about a little piece of paper. As soon as his train pulled into the Linz station, Heinrich understood why the pass mattered so much.

The moment the train stopped, soldiers dressed in the distinctive black uniform of the SS began ordering passengers to line up. Men had to show their pass. When my father showed them his paperwork they waved him through. Nothing could have prepared him for what he saw when he walked through the station doors.

Every lamppost down the entire roadway leading away from the train station had a body hanging from it! All of them were wearing Nazi uniforms. The SS was hanging deserters. Anyone in uniform who didn't have a pass, was immediately executed. Had my father somehow misplaced his little piece of paper, his body would have been hanging with the rest. The German war effort was falling apart and the Nazis were taking drastic action to deter defections.

Every person who came through the station doors stopped in their tracks and gasped at the blackened faces grimacing down at them. One of the female passengers fainted. Another one threw up. It was such a barbaric sight that even hardened soldiers were shaken. In response to how horrifying it was, Heinrich and his fellow passengers clustered together like a flock of frightened sheep. Then the little group started to move slowly down the grisly roadway. They knew that they were being watched by the SS, so they walked with even and deliberate steps, even though every one of them wanted to run. It was the stuff of nightmares.

My father had seen a lot by then: an innocent man being kicked to death, people on a death march, and cattle cars full of families. Of all the things that my father could never have imagined, however, it was his fellow Austrians hanging from the lampposts of his hometown: of Hitler's hometown!

Sadly, the hangings in Linz weren't an isolated occurrence. After the war it was discovered that the German army had executed more than 15,000 of its own troops for desertion and disciplined another 50,000 for insubordination. In the final months of the war, anything less than total commitment was severely punished. The order for this murderous rampage came directly from Adolph Hitler. When it became apparent that the Reich was going down to defeat, he declared that anyone wearing a Nazi uniform had to die for the cause. For the murdered soldiers it wasn't the enemy that took their lives, it was their own army.

While bullets were still plentiful, defectors were simply shot. Once ammunition became scarce, the SS resorted to hanging their victims. These hangings had the added benefit of placing the cost of disloyalty on public display. It allowed the Nazis to once again flaunt their dreadful power over life and death.

Things didn't get any better at the end of that awful road. Since normal civic functions like garbage collection had long since ceased, there was refuse everywhere: clothing, lost shoes, abandoned suitcases, even dead cats and dogs. On every block there were bombed-out buildings leaking the stench of death into the street. Buried deep inside each ruin were the decaying bodies of the residents: most of them the elderly, women and children. By the time he reached his home on Bethlehemstrasse, Heinrich was in tears. At least their building was still standing! He sat on the bottom step and wept. Once he'd managed to pull himself together, he trudged upstairs. His mother and wife collapsed into his arms when they saw him. Heinrich was relieved to see that they were in one piece, but noticed immediately that they'd both become emotional wrecks.

Bombs had been falling for weeks. After the sirens sounded, there were often only minutes to get to the cellar. As a result, the two women lived in a constant state of panic. They were always fully dressed and had a bag packed at all times, so that they could flee at a moment's notice. Their lives had become a never-ending fire drill.

Heinrich did what he could while he was home. Once again he managed to find food, although things out in the countryside had become desperate. With all of their men gone, the women who were left managing their family farms, hid their meager crops in their root cellars. It took a lot of begging and cajoling just to get a few scraps of meat, a couple of eggs and some greens. He tried very hard to enjoy his time at home, but in the back of his mind there was constant worry. How long before his mother and wife died in a bomb blast? How long before a convoy came to collect him and the boys?

A few days into his stay, Heinrich began to think about deserting. He weighed his options. If a truck came for him, he would definitely be sent to the front. He pictured himself lying in a frozen ditch with a bullet in his head. Worse still, he might be at the base when the Russians showed up. Then he would end up being worked to death in some freezing factory or mine. Either way he figured that he was a dead man, so why not run off to the countryside with his mother and wife? Of course, they had nowhere specific to go nor any means of getting there, other than to walk. And now there was the very real danger of running into the SS or of being shot by one of the many fanatical Nazis lurking amongst the Austrian population.

He got the answer to the question of whether or not to desert on the last day of his stay. He was walking down the street when two SS soldiers stopped him. They immediately started to rough him up. Then they demanded to see his pass. Fortunately, he had it with him. Had he left that little piece of paper at home, they would most likely have executed him on the spot. They wrote down his name and address. Then they warned him that he'd better be at the train station at the precise time printed on his pass or else. My father said that he was tempted to ask them: *"Or else what?"* but he didn't dare. Besides he already knew the answer: they would kill him.

My father didn't know if they actually had the ability to check on whether or not he returned to the station on time, but felt that he couldn't risk having them pound on his mother's door. With reluctance, he gave up on the idea of running away and returned to his Czech base. When he got to the train station on his way out of town, the SS were still on duty, checking passes and continuing to behave like the deadly menace that they were. The bodies of the executed soldiers were no longer hanging from the lamp posts, although several nooses still swayed in the breeze.

When Heinrich got back to the Czech Protectorate the boys were so overjoyed to see him that they jumped up and down like little puppies. They'd been terrified without him there and quite lost. He was their big brother and protector. His heart broke all over again thinking about their fate. He didn't tell them about the destruction of Linz or the bodies hanging at the train station. Instead he told them a funny story about his visit to a local farm and a giant pig he saw there. They bought it, or at least they acted as if they did. Mostly they were just glad he was back.

The next day he got the boys involved in a major task. For years lumber and metal scraps had been piling up in a shed behind the shop. Heinrich created a diagram showing where all of the various items needed to be stored and the boys went to work. Raw materials had become impossible to get so Bosch approved of the project. For three days the boys worked tirelessly sorting materials, straightening out bent metal, pulling nails out of reusable lumber and hammering nails until they were straight. When they were done, the storage shed was immaculate and the base had enough supplies to keep functioning.

It was a moment of happiness for the young men, plus the weather had finally become sunny and warm. The trees were a lovely bright green and flowers were blooming everywhere. Heinrich convinced Bosch that the boys had earned a trip outside the base. Reluctantly the base commander gave them a written pass to go to the nearby village. The boys were excited and bounced happily down the road. My father had brought along enough money to buy them a treat, but wondered if anything would be open. He also wondered if the locals would even serve them now that the Nazis were losing the war. At the last minute he decided to avoid the village and took them to a pretty little stream. There they took off their shoes and socks and played in the river.

Sitting on the bank watching them skip stones and hurl water at each other, Heinrich had a thought: Why not make a break for it with the boys? He was familiar with the back roads. He could tell them the truth about the war and their prospects for survival. Then he would ask them if they wanted to escape. They would certainly say yes, if he could assure them that it was safe. That was the problem: my father didn't know if it actually was safe. He didn't know where the Russians were or if the SS was patrolling the area. Above all, he didn't know where they might surrender. It was a plan without a destination. Then he pictured all of them hanging from lampposts. It would be his fault if they died at the hands of the SS. Once again he abandoned the idea of deserting.

Miraculously, the next few months were uneventful, especially in view of what was happening just a few miles away. Since early in 1944 the Allies had been continuously bombing nearby Vienna. By the time the war was over, Vienna had been bombed fifty-two times. The result was that over 37,000 buildings were destroyed, including a significant number of the majestic baroque structures that distinguished the city. In a post war tally it was discovered that only forty-one vehicles of any sort had survived intact. Worst of all, more than 65,000 Viennese citizens lay dead, most of them women and children. It was an absolutely staggering amount of destruction and carnage.

Considering that Vienna was only 135 km away, it was nothing short of amazing that this calamity was neither heard nor felt at the Czech base. Indeed, the only thing that shook Heinrich's world that summer was a letter from his wife announcing that she was expecting. It was the summer of 1944 and her due date was in mid-January of 1945.

This news was simultaneously wonderful and horrifying. Wonderful because they very much wanted to have a family, but horrifying given the circumstances. Resi was already a nervous wreck. Now she would have to go through her pregnancy without enough to eat and constantly running from bombs. Just two weeks later, he received a second letter from her announcing that she'd decided to leave Linz. She would return to Breitenau to be with her mother and sister. The Allies weren't bombing the countryside, so it would be quiet and much safer. Besides she would be with her family. Elisabeth agreed that it was for the best, even though it meant that she would be facing the bombs alone. So, my pregnant mother got on one of the few trains still running and left Linz.

Chapter 7
Flight from Linz

Returning to the countryside would turn out to be a good decision, until it wasn't. Breitenau was definitely more peaceful, plus my mother was now in the care of her family and the ladies of the village. That was the good part. The bad part was that, unbeknownst to the people of Lower Austria, the Russians were about to enter their area by crossing the Hungarian border just a few kilometers to the east. Since that invasion didn't happen right away, my mother had a few peaceful months to enjoy the quiet of the countryside and the fresh produce from the garden. Reports that the Nazis were losing had begun to circulate, which gave her hope that the war might be over by the time her baby was born.

My father received no further letters from either his wife or his mother for the remainder of the war. The mail system hadn't broken down completely, but it had become extremely unreliable. He also never received another pass to go home. He would be trapped inside his Czech base for the remainder of the war. Consequently, he never learned that the summer had been peaceful for his wife. Nor was he aware that on January 19, 1945, she gave birth to their first child: a girl my mother named Elfrieda.

Since all of the hospitals in Vienna had been bombed to rubble, local hospitals like the one in the nearby town of Neunkirchen, were completely full. As a result, my mother ended up giving birth in an unheated tent. A few hours later, the badly overcrowded hospital asked her to leave. Her sister Hilda helped her carry her newborn down the icy road the two kilometers back to Breitenau. She stayed with her mother and sister for a few months after Elfrieda was born, grateful for the help she received from her family. Then the Russians showed up.

Shortly after they captured Hungary, the Russian army crossed into Austria. It was late March of 1945. Since the majority of people living in the small cities and local farming villages were women and children, there was no real fighting. As a result, the Russians were able to quickly take control of the small cities of Eisenstadt and Wiener-Neustadt. The first resistance they encountered was when they reached Vienna. There the remnants of the Nazi army put up a fight that lasted for about a week and resulted in further damage to the already ruined city. By the time the Battle of Vienna was over, only one bridge over the Danube remained standing.

From all accounts, the first wave of Russian soldiers to enter Austria were a well-disciplined fighting machine. The soldiers who were part of the second wave of troops unfortunately were not. This undisciplined mob unleashed a horrendous campaign of looting and rape that would continue unabated for years. Once Vienna had been subdued by the more professional troops, the second wave of marauders moved from building to building stealing anything they could lay their hands on.

Their first goal was to clean out every restaurant, tavern and home of both food and alcohol. Then they stole the furniture. When they raided the homes of the wealthy, they left the residents with nothing but the bare walls. Out in the streets they even took the engines out of vehicles that could no longer be moved. They didn't just steal from the rich though; they even raided the very poor. In my mother's village, Russian troops arrived with trucks and took every stick of furniture that the peasants had in their humble homes. Soon trains loaded with goods could be seen rolling out of Austria, headed for Russia.

The worst thing that the Soviet troops did by far however, was to rape women. They had started that horrendous practice long before they reached Austria. Post-war investigations revealed that they'd also raped Russian, Hungarian, Polish and Ukrainian women. The worst and most aggravated rapes however, were perpetrated against the women of their enemy. They showed them no mercy. The higher the standard of living they encountered, the more viciously the Russian soldiers raped. They were particularly disgusted and enraged by the comfortable houses and the well-stocked kitchens they found in places like Vienna. In these homes they not only raped the women, but often murdered them as well. Assaulting women had become such a standard practice for them that rape became a part of everyday life throughout the Russian-occupied territories.

After the war there was a great deal of discussion about why Russian troops raped and murdered so many women on their way across Europe. It turns out that they'd been egged on by military leaders and Soviet propagandists who saw rape as a valid expression of hatred and therefore good for morale. In addition, soldiers who'd endured considerable hardship and deprivation assumed that raping and pillaging was a right they'd earned. To avoid alienating their troops, Russian commanders turned a blind eye and allowed these offences to continue without punishment.

My mother's little village was not spared this horror. Soon after the Russians entered the area, news from a nearby village told of the brutal gang rape of a mother and her two teenage daughters. When they were done, the soldiers turned everything in the house upside down, before making off with anything of value. The women of Breitenau met the next day to figure out how they might thwart the brutal invaders. After some debate, they decided to hide their women and girls in a large wine cellar buried beneath a vineyard on the outskirts of town. My mother considered that option and decided that it would be a terrible idea to sit in a cold, damp basement with a newborn. Besides the Russians might find them anyway and hurt both herself and the baby. Since she had no friends or relatives elsewhere in Austria, there was only one place she could possibly go and that was Linz.

With reluctance Resi wrote to her mother-in-law to say that she needed to return with little Elfrieda. Because of the dysfunctional mail system, she never found out if Elisabeth actually received her letter. For her part, Elisabeth did receive her daughter-in-law's letter, but her reply never reached my mother. Despite not hearing back from her mother-in-law, Resi set out. With the help of villagers, she managed to scrape up the train fare. Back in the Czech Protectorate Heinrich had no idea that his wife was once again running for her life.

Sometime during the first week of April 1945 my mother boarded a train headed for Linz. She had a suitcase in one hand and her three-month-old baby on her other arm. A few local women were already in the carriage when she boarded. Just before the doors closed, a dozen Russian soldiers got into their car. Inside Resi's suitcase was a large sausage; a generous gift from a neighbor. As time went on the tantalizing smell of the sausage began to waft through the coach. The hungry Russians were soon staring at her. She avoided eye contact and focused her attention on my sister.

Halfway through the journey, the train came to a standstill and remained stalled for over an hour. The longer they were stopped the more obvious the smell of the sausage became. Finally, one of the soldiers walked over and kicked her suitcase. He said something in Russian. My mother put my sister down, opened her suitcase and gave him the sausage. The Russians laughed at her while they ate it. A few minutes later the train started to move again. At the next stop the soldiers got off and everyone breathed a sigh of relief. The train rolled on for another hour then stopped once more. This time they were stalled for over forty-five minutes.

Meanwhile in Linz, Elisabeth had been preparing for the arrival of her grandchild. For weeks she'd been unraveling old sweaters to knit new clothes for the baby. Then she borrowed a crib and a carriage from a neighbor who no longer needed them. She walked to the train station the day before the supposed arrival, just to check the schedule. Since she'd only ever received one letter from my mother, my grandmother was going on assumptions. An hour before the arrival time, my grandmother walked through the deserted streets to meet the train that she hoped would be carrying her daughter-in-law and grandchild. Of course, the train never arrived and no one at the station had any idea what had happened. At eleven, the old women at the ticket counter locked the doors, so my grandmother had to wait on the cold, dark platform. Sometime after two in the morning, she gave up and pushed the empty carriage back home.

My mother's train arrived an hour later. An exhausted Resi got off to find the platform deserted, so she started to walk. There was simply no other option. It took her over an hour to go from the train station to the building on Bethlehemstrasse. Thankfully she didn't encounter anyone during her trek through the rubble-filled streets. Every block was in ruins. Halfway through her trek it suddenly occurred to her that the reason she hadn't heard back from her mother-in-law might be that she was dead! Finally, she turned the last corner to see that the grand old apartment building was still standing. Once she was inside the lobby she knew that she'd made it. After a short rest on the bottom step, she dragged herself up the stairs and knocked on her mother-in-law's door.

As soon as Elisabeth saw my mother and the baby she dissolved into tears: she'd feared the worst. She took Elfrieda and helped my mother to sit down. Then she lit a fire. The electricity had been off for weeks. The few tenants left in the building were more or less camping in their apartments, using old-fashioned oil lamps and cooking in their fireplaces. My mother didn't mind. She told me that it felt as though she'd reached a safe haven after her grueling day. Miraculously there were no air raids the next day, so my mother rested while Elisabeth took care of the baby.

Unfortunately, it was the worst possible time to be in Linz. The Allied bombing raids, which had been going on for about a year, reached a crescendo during the last weeks of the war. The Allies had previously obliterated the Herman Goering steel plant on the banks of the Danube. In the final weeks of the war they bombed all of the remaining industrial sites in Linz, plus key docks, bridges and rail lines. To finish the job, the Allies firebombed Linz. This wasn't as thorough a firebombing as had been inflicted on Dresden, where the entire city, and most of the population, had been completely incinerated. It was none-the-less brutal and further traumatized the remaining residents.

Why were the Allies so keen on destroying Linz? It was in part because Linz was the steel city of Austria. The Allies wanted to ensure that the Reich's entire industrial mechanism had been fully disabled. The other reason for the intense bombing of this relatively small city was purely symbolic: Linz was Hitler's hometown. He'd drawn up elaborate plans for a major art museum in the inner city. There the Nazis planned to display the many art treasures that they'd stolen from the Jewish people. Linz was also earmarked as the location of the massive mausoleum where the Fuhrer would be laid to rest. While they didn't bomb Linz as thoroughly as they did Vienna or the major German cities, there was none-the-less a lot of destruction.

The bombing raids that my mother and grandmother endured must have been extremely harrowing. After the war, researchers estimated that the average Allied bombing run released energy equivalent to 300 lightning strikes. The bombing raids of large German cities like Hanover and Dresden were so intense that they sent shock waves all the way to the edge of space, in some instances briefly weakening the ionosphere, which is the outermost layer of the Earth's atmosphere. The raids inflicted on Linz weren't nearly as intense as that, but were just as terrifying and very deadly. In total the city lost 12,084 buildings and 1,679 citizens as a consequence of 120,000 tons of both explosive and incendiary bombs being dropped on the city.

Because of the constant air raids, those last weeks of the war found my mother and grandmother racing to the cellar almost every day. Sometimes they sat in the dark and heard only distant rumbling. On other days their building shook so violently that they were certain they were about to be buried. I remember how horrified I was when my mother told me that she always kept Elfrieda inside her coat during those raids in case they were buried. She wanted to know that they would be together in the event that they were killed. I was speechless when she said that. It's hard for anyone who hasn't experienced that level of terror to imagine what she and my grandmother went through. The only good thing about the raids was that they almost always took place during daylight hours. That allowed them to develop a routine. They ate breakfast early, then packed everything they might need so that they were ready to run. After surviving weeks and weeks of intense air raids, my mother and grandmother cautiously allowed themselves to believe that they just might survive.

Unfortunately, many of Linz's downtown buildings weren't as fortunate as theirs. By the spring of 1945 there were partially collapsed buildings everywhere. After each bombing raid, refugees from damaged buildings took shelter in any empty apartment they could find. From time to time, there were strangers living inside the building on Bethlehemstrasse. People even sheltered in the stair wells and on the landings. Elisabeth shared what little food she had with these unfortunate folks and took many into her apartment. They never stayed around for very long though. Most fled to the countryside as soon as they were able to find a way to get out of town.

Chapter 8
The SS Death Pact

Back in the Czech Protectorate, trucks never did come to take my father and the boys to the front, for the simple reason that there no longer was a front to take anyone to. The entire German army was in full retreat, not to mention that those who might have come to collect them, were now on the run themselves. With the probability of being sent into battle gone, the challenge became evading capture by the Russians. Since the remaining Nazis at the base never provided an honest report about how the war was actually going, Heinrich knew that he had to find a way to speak with Jaroslav.

Given the growing risk of defections, the three Nazis who were left in the office had recently made it impossible for anyone to leave the base. The gates that had always been open during the day, where now permanently locked. In order to get out, my father had to invent an excuse. So, he lied to Bosch, saying that he needed to help a farmer fix his tractor. The base was still reliant on the locals for food, so Bosch reluctantly agreed. This time he gave my father a pass.

When my father asked why he needed a pass just to visit a local farm, Bosch was evasive, saying something like you never know who you're going to run into. Was this a hint that the SS was patrolling the area? Jaroslav would know. With his pass in his pocket Heinrich biked into the countryside. In his rucksack were tools and fake tractor parts. Jaroslav was thrilled to see him. They pretended to work on his equipment for a while, just in case anyone was watching. After a while, they went into the house to talk. It was the first week of April 1945.

The update Heinrich got from his friend threw him into a total panic. The Germans were in full retreat and Allied ground forces were advancing rapidly. Unfortunately, the Russians were moving just as fast. Their troops were already deep into what would become East Germany. He also learned that the Russians had taken over Hungary and worse, had established themselves as the occupiers of eastern Austria. That meant his wife and newborn child were in the Russian zone!

Since he didn't know that Resi and the baby had fled to Linz, Heinrich now feared that he wouldn't be able to reunite with them. To add to his worries, he learned that the Russian army was already inside the Czech provinces. Jaroslav didn't know their exact location but assumed that they would soon be advancing towards the Austrian border. How long before the base was in Soviet hands? Jaroslav wasn't sure. He stated flatly that he and his family would stay no matter what happened since the farm was their ancestral home. They would tolerate the Russians and hope that they would leave the farmers in peace.

My father biked back to the base with his head full of worries. He worried about his wife and child, who he believed were trapped in the Russian zone. He worried about his mother, who he assumed was alone in her apartment in Linz. He fretted about what would happen to the boys if they were captured by the advancing Soviets. Lastly, he worried about himself. He'd managed to evade the war thus far, but feared that his luck was about to run out.

Even though Jaroslav had assured him that the end of the war was imminent, Gerhard Bosch continued to pretend that everything was fine, so the service center carried on. By now Heinrich had the boys well trained. They did quasi-military exercises in the morning, which the lads really enjoyed. After lunch they helped out in the metal and engine shops for the remainder of the day.

They'd long since outgrown their original clothes and Bosch had somehow managed to find them adult uniforms. He'd even found them boots. When they put on their new gear, they seemed very pleased with themselves. Heinrich marveled at how grown-up they suddenly looked. Then he said a prayer that they'd never have to wear their new outfits into battle.

My father's strategy was to carry on as usual until Jaroslav told him that the Russians were closing in. Then he would hit the road with the boys. He didn't tell them about his plan in case they were accidentally overheard discussing it. The only piece of good news Jaroslav managed to pass along to him during a delivery to the base, was that the Americans were rapidly advancing towards Linz. Unfortunately, Jaroslav had not heard about any surrender camp close enough to be reached on foot. All of Heinrich's hopes for survival were pinned on somehow reaching the Americans.

During my father's last weeks at the base, fewer and fewer items arrived to be repaired. One of the last jobs they got was a truckload of damaged airplane wings that appeared to be from small fighter planes. The wings were badly dented and full of bullet holes. It was clear that the Nazis had been reduced to cobbling together pieces of scrap. My father didn't know where the damaged wings came from and he didn't ask.

He organized the boys into teams: Wolfgang and Ernst cut out the damaged sections; Fritz and Wilhelm measured the holes and cut metal patches. Heinrich welded the new pieces into place, then Leo and Dieter sanded the patches until they were smooth. They finished the entire job in a week. Bosch was so pleased with the boys' work that he personally came to the metal shop to thank them. For the young men, it was a moment of triumph. Only a few months earlier they'd arrived as frightened children; now they felt like adults. My father was very proud of them and more determined than ever to get them out alive.

Unfortunately, the Nazis themselves remained a clear and present danger. The more the German war effort fell apart, the more the SS focused their attention on policing the remaining troops. During the last months of the war, they patrolled train stations, set up roadblocks, and generally terrorized the already traumatized population. After the war, it was discovered that the SS had even executed entire families simply because they'd dared to walk away from a bombed-out city. That campaign of terror arrived at the base in the form of a thirty-five-year-old SS lieutenant named Kurt Lutz. It was the second week of April 1945.

Lutz's arrival was heralded with great fanfare. Bosch made everyone line up to be inspected, which was something that hadn't happened during the entire war. This little piece of window dressing led Heinrich to conclude that this young man had some sort of special clout. During his first hour at the base, Lutz took possession of the keys to every lock. From that moment onward, no one could leave without his permission.

It was immediately apparent that Lt. Lutz was very proud to be wearing the distinctive black uniform of the SS. He could be heard telling and retelling the story of how he'd been promoted after masterminding an attack that had destroyed an entire Russian patrol. He went on and on about his skill and bravery to anyone who would listen. The people at the base didn't necessarily believe his grandiose tale, but they listened attentively because he was SS and was therefore, someone to be feared. It soon became apparent that Gerhard Bosch was afraid of him, too.

On his second day there, Lutz made everyone muster in full uniform at 6:00 am. By now the service center had no actual soldiers left. In fact, the only people in uniform that morning were my father, the six boys, the two mechanics and the two Nazis who worked in the office with Bosch. The only other people at the base were Czech civilians. Lutz began by announcing that the base had been run with too much laxity. He told the tiny assembly that their number one job was to be ready to fight for the Fuhrer. Then he drilled them for two hours, which was totally ridiculous since the base no longer had either rifles or ammunition.

It didn't take long for Lt. Kurt Lutz to figure out that most of the people at the base weren't warrior material. The two guys from the office begged off with the excuse that they had important work to do. The two mechanics did the same. Lutz also came to understand that my father was one of the few people who made the place function. Having discounted all of the adults he turned his attention to the six boys. His new mission became to whip them into shape.

At first the boys idolized Lutz. He was extremely tall and very good-looking: the picture of the blond, blue-eyed Aryan soldier. His stylish black SS uniform had cool medals and insignia they'd never seen before. When he wasn't drilling the boys, they pestered him for stories about his war experiences. Their attention flattered Lutz and helped reduce the danger inherent in the situation. Unfortunately, this convivial atmosphere only lasted a few days before things took a turn for the worse.

Lutz had been instructing the boys in hand-to-hand combat. Unfortunately, the techniques he was teaching were too advanced for them. When they failed to hit each other hard enough, he berated them. Soon they were tackling each other more aggressively. Suddenly, Wolfgang was on the ground, clutching his right shoulder and howling with pain. Lutz stormed over in a rage and kicked him in the gut with his one of his huge boots. Then he hauled the crying lad up by his good shoulder and shouted insults at him. The rest of the boys watched in horror. They'd never seen such violence and it frightened them. Wolfgang's shoulder had been dislocated so badly that his right arm dangled limply. No one at the base could fix it, so one of the mechanics had to drive him to the hospital near Brno. That incident changed the entire dynamic. The boys were now terrified of Lutz

After that, Kurt Lutz became cold and downright mean to them. He was a bully who had found a defenseless group of children to abuse. He started to drill the five remaining lads relentlessly. He constantly berated them and shouted that they weren't battle ready. If any of them showed the slightest sign of weakness he dressed them down with personal insults. After two days of this, Leo fell apart. He'd always been the smallest and slightest of the boys; now he was in tears. My father saw this happen from inside the metal shop. He wanted to rush out and tell Lutz to back off, but realized that his intervention could very well backfire.

So, Heinrich went to Bosch, but the gutless base commander just shrugged. He even suggested that maybe the boys needed to be hardened for what lay ahead. My father wanted to shout at him; *"You know damn well that the war is lost!"* but somehow managed to stop himself. If Bosch wasn't going to stand up to the insane Lutz, my father felt that he needed to figure out a way to neutralize him.

The next day Heinrich started a casual conversation with Lutz in the dining hall. He revealed that he'd met Hitler in person and that Reich's Fuhrer had personally handed him an exclusive copy of *Mein Kampf*. This got his attention. Of all the things that SS Lieutenant Kurt Lutz most wanted, it was to meet Adolph Hitler in person and receive exactly such a copy of *Mein Kampf* for himself.

Then my father told him a series of lies. He told Lutz that he was from a family of top industrialists. He invented a fake uncle and a fake industry name. He told Lutz that as soon the Nazis won the war, he would be going home to a great position in this mythical family business. My father's story went on in great detail and Lutz seemed to be buying it. To put the icing on the cake my father told Lutz that he was exactly the kind of guy his industrialist family would want to employ. Heinrich would put in a good word for him once the war was over. Before he left, my father leaned in to Lutz and told him to keep it all under his hat since no one at the base knew about his family connections.

As he walked away from that exchange my father reflected on the extent to which the war had made a liar out of him. He had to profess undying love for Adolph Hitler. He had to say that he hated the Jews. He even had to pretend that he believed the Nazis were winning the war, even though no one at the base had received a pay check in months. He suddenly realized that he'd been lying for years just to stay alive. He just hoped that Kurt Lutz would somehow buy this particular lie and be more restrained with the boys. For a few days it actually seemed to be working since Lutz was more decent. Sadly, SS Lt. Kurt Lutz simply could not keep his demons in check and once again his worst impulses took control.

It happened while he was drilling the five remaining boys in the yard. After a couple of hours, poor Leopold fell apart again. He simply wasn't cut out for war. When Leo started to cry, Lutz did a despicable thing. He stood him in the center of a circle and ordered his four friends to throw stones at him. The boys were horrified and tossed their stones lamely. On seeing that the boys weren't throwing their stones hard enough, Lutz started to scream at them, his face red with fury. This terrified Leo so thoroughly that he fled. He only managed to run a few steps before Lutz shot him in the back with his revolver. The impact knocked Leo onto his face. Lutz immediately ran over, but it wasn't to check on the dying boy. Instead he stood over him, raised his gun in the air and let out a horrific victory scream.

My father didn't witness the unspeakable incident. By the time he got to the yard, Lutz had gone off to hide and the boys were crying hysterically. Dieter, who was Leo's best friend, lay on the ground sobbing uncontrollably. My father said that he totally broke down at the sight of Leo lying in the dirt with a bloody hole in his back. He had developed a strong bond with young Leo. Seeing him lying dead in the dirt was beyond horrendous!

Heinrich struggled to regain his composure as he gathered the boys around to say a prayer for their fallen friend. They were so traumatized that they could barely utter the words: they just mumbled and cried. Then he took them to their barrack, drew the shades and made them lie down for a rest. Would they ever recover? Once he saw that they'd begun to calm down, my father went to his locker to get his pistol. He admitted to me that it was his intention to kill Kurt Lutz.

Before he made it out of the locker room, Gerhard Bosch and his top lieutenant, Helmut Meyer, intercepted him. They grabbed his arms and made him put his pistol back in his locker. Then they started to talk him down. Bosch was upset, yet he almost seemed to be defending Lutz. *"Yes, it was terrible. No, there was no excuse for killing the boy. Of course, the other boys will no longer be under his control. No, nothing further like that will happen."* He went on like that for a while before he finally spit it out. After a momentary silence, he shrugged his shoulders and said that there was nothing he could do because Kurt Lutz had been given the right to kill anyone he chose.

My father said that that revelation rendered him speechless. Bosch went on to say that the SS had orders from the top to do away with anyone who failed to support the Reich. That certainly explained why everyone at the base was terrified of Lutz. Gerhard Bosch locked eyes with my father until he saw that he fully comprehended their predicament. My father was stunned by how brazenly the Nazis were killing their own people. He sat down on the bench by his locker, barely able to think. He'd assumed that his greatest challenge would be trekking out of the Protectorate ahead of the Russians. Now he realized that he and the boys might not even make it past the gates. Lutz might just decide to kill them all, rather than let the Russians take them.

Then Bosch said that he had a plan. He was going to be all jolly and friendly with Lutz. He was going to tell him that he'd smoothed the whole thing over and that no one was ever going to mention the shooting. He assured my father that everything would be fine. Heinrich hated that Lutz was getting away with murder, but realized that he was powerless to do anything. Even if he did manage to put a bullet into Lutz's skull, the three remaining Nazis in the office would most likely retaliate by killing both him and the boys. He didn't want to give them that provocation. My father admitted to me that he totally broke down after Bosch and Meyer left. The insanity and evil of the war had finally taken his last shred of composure.

Early the next morning Helmut Meyer came to the barrack to tell my father that Leo's body had been buried in the cemetery behind a nearby church. My father had wanted a proper burial that the boys could attend, to give them some sense of closure. Clearly the three Nazis in the office had other ideas: they had wanted the body to disappear. Heinrich doubted that poor Leo actually was in a proper grave, so he asked if the boys might be allowed to visit the cemetery to say a few prayers. Helmut Meyer told him that this wasn't possible but gave no explanation. Heinrich concluded with a heavy heart that they'd most likely disposed of the body somewhere in the woods.

As Helmut turned to leave, my father noticed that his eyes were red, as if he'd been crying. Surely he hadn't been crying over poor Leo! Then why were they red? Heinrich didn't learn the answer to that question until the next day. It turns out that just an hour earlier the base had received a wireless report that Adolph Hitler had been found dead. His charred remains had been discovered on the ground just outside his bunker in Berlin. He'd committed suicide in the early hours of April 30th.

For the remainder of that day the base was silent. No one came to the gates, not even the farmers who normally made deliveries. They'd probably heard of Hitler's death and were thinking that it was best to steer clear now that the Nazis were on the verge of defeat. No one moved around inside the base either. Lutz stayed undercover; in fact, my father never saw him again. The boys stayed in their beds, lounging listlessly. Wolfgang, who had missed the horror of the shooting, lay in his cot, quietly nursing his injured shoulder.

Sometime in the middle of the afternoon, Heinrich finally told the boys that the Germans had lost the war and were about to surrender. They were so depressed over the death of their friend that they barely reacted. Deep down they probably knew that the war wasn't going as advertised. Then my father retreated to the deserted metal shop to try to figure out what to do next. He wanted to leave immediately but had no idea how to get past the locked gates without being seen.

Around dinner time my father went to the kitchen to get food for himself and the boys. The kitchen was deserted. The Czech ladies who'd been working there just the day before were gone. So was most of the food. Heinrich found some bread, cheese, and apples and returned to the barrack. He told the boys that something was afoot and that they should stay inside. They were so traumatized that none of them reacted or said a word.

Before they went to sleep, Heinrich pushed their beds together to make the boys feel safer. Just as he was about to lay down my father pictured Lutz coming to shoot them in the middle of the night, so he went to get his firearm. Then he barricaded the door with a heavy chest. He resolved that if anyone tried to get to them, he would put the six bullets languishing in his pistol to good use.

Chapter 9
Exodus

Just after three in the morning on the first of May 1945, Jaroslav Dura and his wife Ivana were jolted awake by furious barking. This was followed by two shots and loud yelping. Jaroslav bolted to the window. In the dark he made out the silhouettes of four men walking down the road beside his farmhouse. One of them was extremely tall. It was Lutz! It only took Jaroslav a few seconds to figure out what was going on. The four remaining Nazis at the base were deserting. That meant that the base was unguarded. He rushed to get dressed.

A few minutes later he was biking furiously down the road. Jaroslav would have rather driven his truck, but the farm had long since run out of petrol. He figured that it was probably better to be biking anyway. That way he could easily dive into the woods if he ran into anyone. Fortunately, the roads were empty. He reached the base just before four to find the gate locked. He was furious that the selfish Nazi bastards had left the others trapped inside, vulnerable to being captured. He wondered why they hadn't taken the rest of the men with them, especially the boys.

Jaroslav rushed to the fence nearest the barracks and began to shout: *"The Nazis are gone! Get the bolt cutters and open the gate!"*. My father jumped up and ran to the shop. While he was cutting the lock, Jaroslav informed Heinrich of Hitler's death the day before. That news was shocking enough, but even more distressing was the news that the Russians had taken possession of nearby Brno. That put them within 20 km of the base! Jaroslav was positive that the Russians would be at their gate by daybreak, if not sooner. Then he shared a significant piece of information that he'd gleaned from a wireless broadcast. He told Heinrich the approximate location of a temporary Americans surrender camp just inside the Austrian border. On a scrap of paper, he drew a rough map. Heinrich did the calculations: the Russians were 20 km to the east and the Americans were 98 km to the southwest.

My father needed no further incentive to leave. This was what he'd been waiting for: a chance to get home to his family and a chance for the boys to have a life. He mobilized them to get dressed and gather whatever food they could find. Then he faced a dilemma: whether to wear his overalls or his uniform. He estimated the distance from the base to the Austrian border to be about a two-day walk. The overalls wouldn't provide much protection during the night or if they had to crawl through any sort of underbrush. Besides the boys would be wearing their Nazi uniforms. In solidarity with them he put on his uniform, holster and pistol. Within twenty minutes of Jaroslav's arrival he and the boys were walking down the road.

They weren't alone. My father and the five boys were joined by the two mechanics from the engine shop. Like Heinrich, Jonas Eisner and Louis Ryker had also managed to evade the war. At one time there'd been more than two hundred enlisted personnel at the base. Now these eight souls walking down the dark road were the only ones left. At least Lutz hadn't killed them. In the end, the SS lieutenant who'd been prepared to kill anyone who deserted had decided to save his own skin by deserting. If they had any real honor, Heinrich thought, Lutz and the three others would have shot themselves.

Jaroslav accompanied them until they reached the road leading to the Dura farm. While they walked he told my father everything he knew about useful shortcuts and intersections to avoid. Before he turned off, he and my father embraced. Both men cried. They'd become brothers. Heinrich had sat in the warmth of the Dura family kitchen so many times over the years. They'd shared food and more than a few laughs. Both men sensed that they'd never see each other again. A terrible iron curtain would soon fall between Czechoslovakia and Austria, blocking all contact for decades.

It broke my father's heart to watch his friend ride away. Then he said a silent prayer for the safety of the Dura family. Jaroslav had undoubtedly saved their lives. If he hadn't awakened them, they would have been in their beds when the Russians arrived at daybreak. A chill ran down Heinrich's spine when he thought about how close they'd come to being enslaved.

Although they'd started their trek in the dark, it soon became light. This was not a welcome change, since the darkness had given them a degree of cover. Daylight made them feel vulnerable, so they started walking faster. At one point, my father noticed a baby carriage in a ditch. He pulled it out and saw that it was still useable. He put it on the road and tossed in his jacket and the small bag he'd been carrying. Soon others tossed in their coats and whatever else they'd been carrying, including a battered rifle that Jonas Eisner had brought along. My father wondered if he even had bullets for the thing, since no one at the base had seen ammunition in months. Someone in the group made a wry comment about the absurdity of a group of Nazis walking through the woods pushing a baby carriage. Everyone chuckled. It was a much-needed bit of comic relief. After a couple of hours one of the wheels started to wobble so badly that my father had to ditch the carriage and make everybody lug their stuff again. No one minded. Carrying a coat or small parcel was the least of their worries.

The great unknown aspect of their journey through the Czech countryside was who they might encounter, so the group developed a plan. It was decided that no one would walk in the middle of the road; instead they would stick to the sides. That way it would be easy to dive into the underbrush. They also divided themselves into three groups. One of them would walk several meters out in front and one of them would walk several meters to the rear. The rest would stay near the middle. That way anyone who came along would only see one person while the others hid. Every half hour or so, they switched positions. Throughout the morning they didn't see a soul. The farmers who normally used those roads had clearly decided to stay home.

Around noon, the group stopped for a bathroom break and to share what little food they had left; then they resumed walking. No one wanted to stop. My father checked Jaroslav's map. He reckoned that if they walked through the night, they would be in Austria by mid-morning. Now that they were actually moving towards freedom, my father felt as though it couldn't possibly be happening. He hardly dared imagine that they were actually going to make it, although he told the boys that they would soon be safe. They only managed weak smiles. They were still completely numb from the shock of Leo's death.

In the middle of the afternoon my father noticed a sign announcing a town he'd once visited while searching for his ancestral papers. This town was just north of the road they were currently on and was located on the main route leading to Prague. Just before they reached the actual intersection, Wilhelm, who was bringing up the rear, whistled twice. That was their signal that someone was coming. Everyone dove into the woods. Seconds later a convoy of four Russian armored vehicles rumbled past. They were coming from the direction of Brno. At the intersection they turned north and headed towards Prague. A cold shiver ran through Heinrich. He wondered if these weren't the very vehicles to have visited their base that morning, looking for people to arrest.

Apparently, the Russians hadn't spotted them, because their vehicles rolled by without pause. Could more Russians be coming along? It was impossible to know, so they stayed hidden for a while longer, their hearts pounding. Finally, my father crept through the forest towards the road leading to Prague. Heinrich watched it for almost twenty minutes. Then he went back to help the group create a new plan. They would leave the woods in pairs. That way if any two of them were captured the rest would be able to stay hidden. The others were to come out of hiding only if they heard the all-clear signal. My father and

Jonas went first. Luckily there weren't any more Russian vehicles in the area. Because they were being cautious, it took over an hour for everyone to cross the intersection. Finally, they were all once again walking towards the Austrian border.

The encounter with the Russian convoy had shaken them. Everyone acted calm, but deep down each of them knew that there was still a good chance that they might be captured. When night fell, Jonas and Louis announced that they intended to keep going. My father would have liked to keep walking too, but felt that he had to let the boys rest, especially Wolfgang who was in a lot of pain. Shortly before midnight, he led them into the forest to sleep. Just before sunrise, he and the boys were once again back on the road.

When Jaroslav described the route, he said that they would eventually reach a small river with a concrete bridge. When they got to that spot, the bridge was gone. It had been bombed into large chunks that lay in the stream and in heaps on both banks. That meant that they would have to wade through the waist-deep water. After hiding in the woods for a while to observe the scene, my father organized the boys. He would go first to find decent footing. If it was safe, they would follow. When he was able to cross easily, he motioned for them to join him. Ernst and Wilhelm crossed next. They had just made it across when they heard the sound of an approaching plane. Wolfgang and Fritz were in the middle of the stream. Dieter was still back on the far bank.

My father shouted at everyone to take cover. He, Ernst and Wilhelm hid behind some large concrete blocks. Wolfgang and Fritz froze in the middle of the stream. Dieter ran back to hide behind the rubble on his side of the river. Suddenly the plane was on them. It was a small German prop job similar to the ones that Heinrich had repaired dozens of times. The small plane swooped down low. When it was directly overhead the pilot reached out his window and manually dropped a small explosive into the pile of broken concrete on the far side of the river. There was a deafening explosion that sent chunks flying everywhere. Then there was silence. Would the plane be back? Where there more in the area?

Heinrich told Ernst and Wilhelm to stay where they were, then he rushed to fetch Wolfgang and Fritz who were standing catatonic in the waist-deep water. After he'd helped them to shore, he went to get Dieter. As soon as he was within a few feet of the explosion site, my father knew that Dieter had not survived. There was blood everywhere. Dieter was lying face up, with a gaping hole where his chest had been. The pilot must have seen the lad clearly since he'd more or less tossed the explosive right at him.

My father immediately re-crossed the river. He said nothing to his four remaining charges except that they needed to move fast. No one could bear to talk about what had just happened, so they trekked on in stony silence. All of them were crying. Despite the terrible tragedy of Dieter's death, stopping was not an option: they had to keep moving, especially since the SS was actively hunting deserters.

It was now just the five of them. Heinrich had hoped to reach the Austrian border by mid-afternoon, but he no longer had any idea where they were. For several hours they trudged on in a state of deep depression. No one had said a word since the river: it was just too awful to discuss. Then they heard voices. My father told the boys to hide while he crept along the edge of the forest to see what lay ahead. In an open field Heinrich saw military vehicles arranged in a large circle. Hanging from one of the trucks was a tattered American flag.

My father said that it was the most glorious thing he'd ever seen. But was it real? Perhaps the Nazis had created a decoy to capture people like him. He waited for a sign that it really was the Americans. After about twenty minutes a soldier came to get something from one of the vehicles. He rooted around in the back of one of the trucks, then shouted something that sounded like English. Heinrich went back to tell the boys. They agreed on a new plan. He would surrender alone. If it was safe, he would call their names. If they didn't hear him call their names they were to stay hidden, then resume walking south after dark. He deliberately didn't say goodbye to them. Then he walked towards the circle of trucks to surrender.

During their trek out of the Czech Protectorate, Jonas and Louis had thrown their badges and insignia into the forest. Later on, they'd actually turned their coats inside out so as not to look like the enemy. My father did none of that. He'd been in the military and would stay in his uniform. He did, however, remove his pistol and hold it over his head. In it were the six bullets he'd been given all those years ago. Then he walked towards the encampment. Around one side of the circle of trucks there was a makeshift entrance with two armed guards. He walked slowly towards them but stopped when they called out to him. Then they signaled for him to proceed. He handed them his gun. The moment they had it, they lowered their rifles. A third GI came out to frisk him. When he was done, he motioned to my father to enter the camp.

Heinrich spoke no English, so he asked them: *"Sprechen Sie Deutch?"* They understood what he was asking, but shook their heads and said: *"No, we don't speak German."* My father then used sign language to convey that there were others in the woods. They looked puzzled, so he cupped his hands to indicate that he wanted to shout to someone. They seemed okay with it so he shouted the boys' names as loudly as he could. Then all of them turned to look in the direction of the woods. A few minutes later the four young men came into view. Heinrich gestured for them to come. They started walking faster. Heinrich wanted to jump for joy but remained calm. The boys acted calm too. They were searched, and minutes later the five of them were inside the American compound.

Chapter 10
Safe Surrender

The encampment was little more than a circle of trucks and a few tents. On the far side there were some hastily dug latrines. The grass inside the circle had been trampled down, which indicated that the camp had been there for a while. On either side of the field there were mounds of straw. About a dozen guys in Nazi uniforms were sitting on each pile. Heinrich didn't recognize any of them and wondered if Jonas and Louis had ever made it to this particular camp. Perhaps they'd seen it but had chosen to keep walking south.

The GI from the gate signaled to my father and the boys to go sit on one of the straw mounds. A few minutes later he came around with a clipboard seeking simple information like name and home address. When he got to Wolfgang he noticed that he had his shoulder in a sling and appeared to be in pain. He called out across the site. A few minutes later a soldier emerged from a small tent to escort Wolfgang away. When my father looked concerned the young GI patted his hand and said something that sounded reassuring. About twenty minutes later Wolfgang reappeared with a clean sling and a relieved expression. The medic had changed his dressing and given him something for his pain.

Then someone stepped out of the big tent and waved at everyone on their side of the field to come forward. People got up reluctantly. Were they going to be interrogated? Would they be placed in handcuffs? Beaten perhaps? They walked forward slowly. When they got inside the tent they were shocked to see that they were about to be fed! My father wanted to hug the nearest GI but restrained himself. Everyone else acted nonchalant too, although my father knew that they were all equally amazed. Were the Germans treating captured American and Russian troops like this? It seemed unlikely since they weren't even treating their own people with humanity.

The chow line was spartan. There were eggs, made from some kind of powder and corned beef taken from huge cans that were stacked everywhere. No one said a word as they progressed down the line. Most were stunned that the enemy was feeding them instead of humiliating them in some way. Soon they were outside eating. It tasted like heaven. About thirty minutes later a soldier collected their plates and spoons and motioned to them that they could use the latrines. Slowly people realized they could get up and walk around. In fact, there was no fencing anywhere. Anyone could slip out between the parked vehicles. Of course, no one left because they were exactly where they wanted to be. When night fell, two GIs from the big tent put out a large container of water for everyone to have a drink. Just before dark someone did a final head count. Then the place went quiet.

Heinrich stayed awake for a while to make sure the boys were all right. They had been in a terrible state since the deaths of their two friends. The only good thing about their emotional exhaustion was that it caused them to fall asleep quickly. As my father watched them resting peacefully, he finally allowed himself to relax a bit. He was heartsick that Leo and Dieter hadn't made it, but was grateful that Fritz, Ernst, Wolfgang and Wilhelm hadn't been killed. They could all have very easily perished at the hands of either the Nazis or the Russians. Then he heard it: the muffled sound of grown men crying. They'd held it in while they were being watched, but under the cover of darkness it could be contained no more. Hearing them weep made Heinrich cry too. It was cathartic. Soon all of the exhausted men were asleep.

In the morning they got the same food from the same people. No one was complaining. A few minutes later four trucks rolled up and a new GI started calling out the names of various destinations. My father told me that he could scarcely believe it. Were their captors actually going to drive them home? He was incredulous. The Americans were living up to their promise of letting their enemies go free. Like the Finns, they were demonstrating their civility and their humanity. After years of witnessing the hateful and downright murderous behavior of his fellow Nazis, the decency of the Americans was shocking.

Several decades later, while we were living in Canada, my father met an Austrian soldier who'd been captured by the Russians. His tale of capture was very different. Carl related that the Russians had taken about a hundred of them to a deserted stadium. There they were starved for days in a dark dungeon. In that dungeon they weren't allowed to go to the bathroom or to wash. On the third day they opened the doors to the sports field. In the middle of the field there was a long table full of food. The filthy, unkempt men rushed to the table and started to stuff themselves. Since there wasn't enough food for everyone, fights broke out. The horrible scene was filmed by the Soviets so that they could show the Russian people that the Nazis were nothing more than animals. After that, the entire group was thrown into leg irons and taken to a work camp in the Ural Mountains. That was the fate that befell an estimated 500,000 Axis soldiers who were captured by the Soviets. They stayed in those forced labor camps until 1956, when the West German and Austrian governments finally negotiated their release. By that time only about 5,000 were still alive. The rest had all been worked to death. A very stark contrast to how the Americans were treating their enemies.

Despite being thrilled at the prospect of going home, Heinrich was sad that he and the boys were to be parted. Over the last year, they'd become close. Only Ernst and Wilhelm joined him in the truck headed for Linz. Wolfgang and Fritz were going to the province of Styria, which they learned was now under British control. He hoped that they would find their families alive and well. After weeks of fear and stress the boys finally had something to be happy about. Naturally there were tears too, because the young men had become such great friends. Despite everything that had transpired they were happy to be seeing the end of the war. My father had made them memorize his address a long time ago. Now he reminded them that they could come to find him if they were ever in trouble. After more tears and final words of farewell, they got into their respective trucks.

Until they started driving through the countryside, my father didn't know the exact location of the surrender camp. Within a few kilometers he started to notice vaguely familiar landmarks. Then he saw a sign that said Freistadt, which is a small town just a few kilometers north of Linz. He suddenly realized that he'd walked almost all the way home! His elation evaporated though, the moment Linz came into view. Freistadt had been intact. The surrounding vineyards had also been undisturbed, but Linz was another matter. All he saw from the back of the truck was dirt and destruction. Fear gripped Heinrich. What if his home was in ruins? What if his family was dead? Where were Resi and the baby? He'd been so preoccupied with escaping that he hadn't had time to think about what he would find if he actually managed to make it home. Now scenes of destruction flew past and he became frantic.

When the truck finally stopped near the train station, Heinrich thanked the soldiers and began to run. He'd already said goodbye to Ernst and Wilhelm. The two of them were from the same Linz suburb and had assured him that they would stay together until they reached their homes. For the next half-hour my father ran, stopping only to catch his breath, then running some more. Finally, he turned the corner on Bethlehemstrasse. The grand old apartment building was still standing! He could scarcely believe it. He rushed through the lobby and up the stairs.

When his mother opened the apartment door, she shrieked and burst into tears. To his amazement, Resi rushed out a minute later. He was immediately locked in their embrace. They continued to scream and cry until the building's remaining tenants opened their doors to see the commotion. Soon a dozen people were crying along with them. They were crying in solidarity with the happiness of the Dolezal family and also because their own sons, husbands and fathers were still missing. The emotional wreckage experienced by the citizens of Linz, perfectly matched the rubble outside. Everything and everybody had been destroyed.

Then Heinrich got to meet his daughter, Elfrieda. She was four months old and blissfully oblivious to the trauma around her. He noted that she had dark, curly hair like her mother and instantly fell in love. Then he slept. Apparently it took him the better part of a week to recover even a modicum of strength. While he'd been in the middle of his escape ordeal he had just kept going. As soon as it was over, Heinrich more or less collapsed. My mother said that he was pale and shockingly thin when he arrived at their door. He had literally become a shadow of his former self. Regardless, he was extremely lucky. It could all have ended so very differently.

Shattered Vienna

Chapter 11
Aftermath

Heinrich Dolezal arrived home on May 4, 1945. A few days later the German high command formally surrendered to the Allies. Although the war in the Pacific would continue until September, the horrendous war in Europe was officially over.

Since there were no functioning newspapers or radio stations, the news had to be carried from person to person. For the next several days, people of all ages could be heard running through the streets shouting: *"The war is over! The war is over!"*. People couldn't stop saying it. By then they no longer cared who'd actually won, they were just happy that their prolonged nightmare had finally ended.

At this point I assumed that we'd arrived at the end of my father's story. Now that the Germans had surrendered to the Allies, the greatest danger was surely behind him. It turns out that I was completely wrong. The most perilous and heartbreaking part of his saga lay just ahead. While it was true that the bombing and shelling had stopped, the citizens of Austria would soon discover that the aftermath would be just as harrowing as the war itself.

Two days after my father's homecoming there was a commotion in the hallway of their building. When Elisabeth opened her door, she was shocked to see that the entire second floor landing was full of people. There were more of them just inside the entrance on the ground floor. They were skin and bones and were all wearing the same dirty, striped pajamas. They were the inmates of the Mauthausen labor camp.

A day or so earlier, 6,000 wretched and abused prisoners had awakened to find that the camp's guards had disappeared. As soon as they were able to open the gates, those who had sufficient strength, started to walk. They had no idea where they were going, they just knew that they wanted to get away from that horrendous place. Some of them wandered into local villages and randomly knocked on doors. Others walked towards nearby farms. The group in their building had walked for the better part of a day to get to Linz.

As soon as they entered the apartment building on Bethlehemstrasse, they lay down. They lay down because they had expended their last shred of energy to get away from that hellhole. Elisabeth and her neighbors gave them water and blankets, but the camp survivors refused all food. After months of near starvation their digestive systems no longer worked. Someone ran to report their arrival to the American military post down the street. The next day two large trucks came to take them for much needed medical care. Each person had to be placed on a stretcher and carried out. Not one of the camp survivors had enough strength to even stand up, let alone walk.

Those who survived the Mauthausen camp were eventually able to tell their story. For years the Nazis had been giving them just enough food to stave off total collapse. While extermination camps like Auschwitz were truly horrific, the suffering was even more acute in places like Mauthausen and Dachau, that were built to extract labor. These were the camps where victims suffered the most and for the longest period of time.

One survivor of Mauthausen recounted that whenever prisoners appeared to be near death they were offered an option. Guards would take them to the rim of the quarry in pairs and tell them to either jump or push the other guy. Apparently the guards found this to be amusing. Even without this extreme form of cruelty, daily life at the quarry was torture. The pit was deep, which made it extremely hard for the emaciated prisoners to drag the gigantic blocks of granite up the steep pathways. To some extent the entire enterprise seemed designed to see just how much people could endure before they finally succumbed.

Of course, the citizens of Linz didn't know the full horrors of the Nazi gulag system just as the war was ending. The full picture of how cruelly the Jewish people and other nationalities had been treated would not be understood for some time. All the citizens of Linz knew for certain in May of 1945 was that the world they had known had come to an end. Most were still in shock after months of devastating bombing raids. With few exceptions, everyone was also mourning the loss of family members.

While Austria was not bombed to the same extent as Germany, there was nonetheless a lot of damage in all of the major cities. In addition to the horrible destruction of Vienna and Linz, Salzburg and Innsbruck had also been bombed extensively. In

Salzburg fifteen air strikes had destroyed almost fifty percent of the city's buildings, especially those near the railway station. In addition, all of the town's bridges were gone, as was the dome of the main cathedral. In total, Salzburg lost 7,600 buildings and 550 inhabitants.

Scenic Innsbruck was not spared either since it was the hub for four major rail lines. To ensure that this important junction was fully disabled, the Allies bombed little Innsbruck twenty-two times over a period of five months. By May of 1945 Innsbruck had lost sixty percent of its buildings and 461 of its citizens lay dead. One result of all this destruction was that there were now millions of displaced people, mostly women and children, living in squalid refugee camps all over the countryside.

In addition to the damage to buildings, roads and bridges, all levels of government had long since collapsed. Important civic functions like garbage collection, water management, power utilities and policing no longer existed. For months after the official end of the war, there was no electricity or running water. Food was also scarce and medical care was non-existent. Just when the beleaguered citizens thought that things could not possibly get any worse, Austria was hit with a drought so severe that the country was thrown into a massive famine. This famine was so bad that the Allies felt compelled to organize 300 million dollars-worth of food aid for the remaining Austrian people. Despite their efforts, over 100,000 Austrians died of starvation in the years immediately after the end of the war. Most of them were the elderly, women and children.

In the midst of this catastrophe, the only good news for the citizens of Linz was that most of their city was in the hands of the US. For a while the Americans had controlled all of the city, but a new agreement gave the land north of the Danube to the Russians. That meant that the spot where my father had surrendered was no longer in American hands. It also meant that the Russians were now just a stone's throw away. Their armed checkpoint could be clearly seen just across the river from downtown.

These were the stark realities that confronted Heinrich upon his return home. Nothing was working and there was no way to earn money or find food. Plus, he now had four mouths to feed. He recalled getting on his bike to ride around the city to take stock of the situation. He barely recognized anything. When he went to the home of his best friend, he found a bombed-out ruin. When he tried to find Aunt Helene's apartment building, there was nothing there but rubble. Block after block looked like that. No one was living at any of the homes he visited. The only sign of order was the presence of American troops, who'd set up small command posts across the city.

After a few days of riding around without finding anything, Heinrich decided to go into business for himself. Directly across the street from their apartment building there was a bombed-out shell of a store. He took over the ruin and hung up a sign that said *Spenglerei (Metal Working Shop)*. Every day he took the tools and supplies that his mother had carefully stored for him across the street to his new shop. Within a few days people started to bring him broken items to fix. A few were even able to pay for his help. Others offered bits of food in exchange for his services. He also started to build things. His first creation was a wooden cart made from scraps of wood and a pair of wheels he'd found. Once he had the cart, he scoured bombed-out buildings to collect copper pipe and other bits of metal that was jutting out of the debris. At a newly establish scrap yard on the edge of town, the proprietor paid him for his haul. He'd started to make money!

A few days into his new venture, two American soldiers sped past my father's shop in a jeep, threw on the brakes, then backed up to check him out. The soldiers were curious to see what he was doing. My father had no idea what they were saying, but he understood what they needed when they showed him their fender. It had come loose. My father quickly reattached the fender. They immediately paid him in US dollars. The next morning the same guys came back with a jeep in need of repairs to its back bumper. While my father worked on their vehicle, the soldiers put up a sign they'd whipped up at their base. It said **Auto Body Shop.**

The next day, American military vehicles started arriving. Soon there were so many cars, trucks and trailers being dropped off that Heinrich had to take over the vacant lot next door. To protect their equipment, the Americans posted a guard. When his mother came to take a look, she was impressed that American soldiers were protecting her son's new business. What my father found most ironic about his new venture was that he'd spent the entire war fixing equipment for the Nazis and was now doing the same thing for the people they'd been fighting!

About a week into his new auto body repair business, the GI who originally discovered him came by with a box of metalworking supplies including coils of solder. These were things that Heinrich wouldn't have otherwise been unable to find. Jim also gave him a small dictionary. It was both English to German and German to English. Then he gifted my father a pad of paper and a pencil. On the pad he wrote down what he needed and by when. Heinrich looked it up and was able to write a reply. So, began his acquisition of the English language.

The only problem with all of this new-found prosperity was that there was practically nothing to buy. The few shops that were open had long lines and almost no food. Elisabeth and Resi were now spending all of their time in endless queues. Most days they came home with very little, and often with nothing at all. So, my father went back to the business he knew had appeal to farmers: building stills.

He hired two enterprising boys to scavenge copper tubing in the ruins. As soon as he had enough parts for at least two stills, he biked into the surrounding countryside to exchange them for food. The strategy worked! Beleaguered farm families were generally unwilling to give anything up, especially given the terrible drought ravaging the country. The potential of increasing their liquor sales however, got them to open their root cellars. By October of 1945 there was finally enough food in the house.

About five months into this chaos the Dolezal household heard another knock on the door. This time it was Walter! The return of her eldest son was such a shock that Elisabeth sank to the floor in a dead faint. He hadn't been heard from in over five years and had been presumed dead. The other reason his mother fainted was that he looked absolutely terrible.

Although his hydrocephalus had been treated, his head was still very swollen, which badly distorted his facial features. He was also so weak that he couldn't stand. He'd been carried to their door by an ambulance team that had found him comatose on a train at the Linz station. His name and address were on a note pinned to his jacket. It would be weeks before Walter was able to tell his story. For now, he needed nourishment and rest. At that point my grandmother had moved into the boys' old room, so that my father, mother and sister could have the master bedroom. When Walter arrived, they created a bed for him in the parlor. He lay there for weeks, slipping in and out of consciousness.

Chapter 12
The Russian Occupation

In addition to the lack of services and food, the other dark cloud that continued to hang over Austria was the presence of the Russians. During the final months of the conflict, the Allies and the Soviets had decided to partition the country into four sections. The French got the western, alpine states, while the British took possession of the rolling countryside in the southern part of the country. The Americans got the states of Salzburg and Upper Austria, which is where most of Linz was located. Unfortunately, the Russians gained control of the flat, eastern region of the country, which held 65% of the country's oil fields and agricultural land.

The Russians, it would turn out, had little interest in managing those rich assets effectively. Whatever local farmers produced was either consumed by the soldiers or shipped back to Russia. The Soviets also had no interest in properly managing the many successful businesses in their section of the country. Within a few years, over five hundred enterprises had become insolvent. If all that wasn't bad enough, the Soviet occupiers continued to rape any woman they encountered, including the elderly and the very young. At the end of the war it was estimated that Russian soldiers had been responsible for over 90% of all crimes committed in the entire country, throughout the years of the occupation. A horrendous legacy.

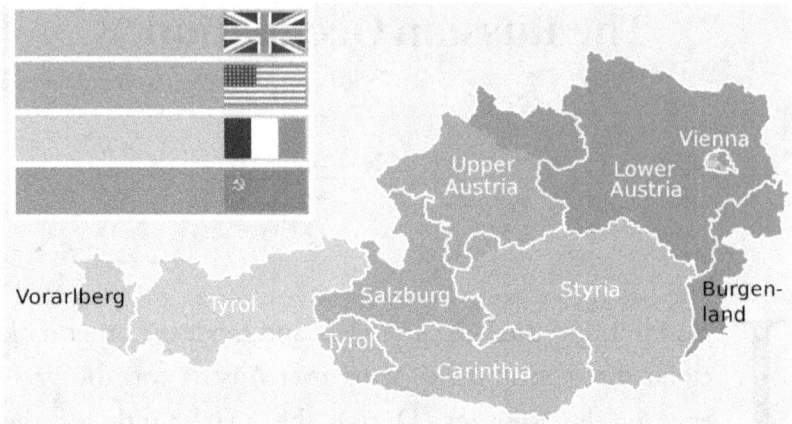

For a long time, Heinrich diligently avoided the Russians, whose guard post could be seen on the other side of the main downtown bridge. Every time he caught sight of their check point, a cold shiver ran down his spine. He could hardly bear to think about how close he'd come to being in their hands. Unfortunately, in the fall of 1947 he ignored his deepest misgivings and ventured into their territory.

It happened because two businessmen brought him a deal that he felt he couldn't refuse. Despite the fact that he'd been working non-stop for almost two years, he was barely able to take care of the people in his household. The offer that he got from Helmut Schneider and Johan Weber was to become the owner of his own motorcycle dealership.

Austria was slowly recovering and people needed transportation. Economical vehicles like Vespas and Mopeds had recently become available and there was growing demand. He would have to pay Helmut and Johan a franchise fee, but would otherwise be the sole owner of the dealership. The prospect of financial independence had real appeal, plus, my father really liked the two guys. They already had a successful shop in the city and showed him their impressive receipts. Heinrich could see that he'd be in a much better position if he owned a thriving business. Since he'd been accumulating American cash for a while, my father had the money needed to invest.

There was just one catch: the dealership his two new friends wanted him to operate was in the Russian part of Linz, just a few blocks north of the Danube. When Heinrich shared his concerns about going into Soviet territory, his new partners assured him that he would receive a special pass that would allow him to freely move back and forth. They both had these special passes and regularly travelled in and out of the Russian zone. To demonstrate just how safe it was, they got him one of those special passes and took him over the bridge to tour the site they'd secured for him. Just as they'd promised, they had no trouble getting back through the Russian checkpoint at the end of their visit.

With that assurance and the encouragement of his mother and wife, my father put his money down and started his new business. For months everything went well. His partners helped him get started and supplied him with bikes. Heinrich hired a mechanic and the shop soon started to service a wide range of vehicles in need of repair. The business was successful from the moment it opened. During his first few weeks at his new location several groups of Russian soldiers dropped by to see what he was doing. My father said that he was surprised by how friendly and polite they were. Their easy manner further calmed his fears.

The summer of 1947 was finally a period of happiness for the Dolezal family. The newly organized local government had started to clear the rubble and re-establish basic services. New businesses had begun to open and people were finally able to find jobs. Walter had recovered his health and had secured a managerial position with a newly formed Austrian department store chain. My grandmother was finally able to buy enough fabric to restart her tailoring business and was once again happily serving customers. And of course, my father was excited about his new business. The happiest person in the family by far though, was my mother, who'd discovered that she was expecting again. This news was greeted with joy by the whole family. After so many years of loss, the prospect of a new baby lifted everyone's spirits.

That's when the unthinkable happened. About two weeks before Christmas the family heard a frantic knock at the door. It was dinner time, so they'd been expecting my father. Instead it was their neighbor from the third floor. Hanna Schmidt had recently started selling baked goods on the downtown bridge over the Danube. Her table was fairly close to the Russian checkpoint. By sheer chance she saw soldiers take my father into custody as he tried to return to the American zone at the end of the day.

Hanna was breathless and talking so fast she could barely be understood. Finally, she calmed down enough to report that she'd seen my father being handcuffed by border guards and placed into the back of a military vehicle. My mother and grandmother were immediately thrown into a state of total panic. Levels of anxiety and dread, that they hadn't felt in years, came flooding back. Thankfully Walter was there to take charge.

He immediately went to look for my father's partners. He found Helmut Schneider at their shop just a few blocks away. Helmut was familiar with the Russian zone and was able to identify where Heinrich was likely being held. It was a former school building that the Russians had turned into a command post. With Helmut's help they formulated a rescue plan. While they were getting organized, Heinrich was sitting in a freezing room with ten other men, who had likewise been arrested without cause. From them he learned their fate. They were to be slave labor in a mine somewhere in the Ural Mountains.

When I asked my father what went through his mind when he heard where they were to be sent, he said that he knew immediately that it was a death sentence, and a dreadful one at that. Working in a mine meant years of back-breaking labor in freezing temperatures with little food. To have this happen, after having successfully evaded the Russians at the end of the war, was absolutely sickening. Above all, my father said that he was furious with himself for having voluntarily gone into their zone. How stupid! As he sat in that room listening to the grown men around him cry, he felt certain that he would never see his family again.

Just after 2:00 am the next morning, my five-months pregnant mother, neighbor Hanna Schmidt and four small children started walking through the frigid streets of Linz headed for the bridge. The group of kids included my sister Elfrieda, who was two, and three other youngsters who were a bit older. They'd been borrowed from families in the building. In a leather satchel, my mother carried a large bottle of Schnapps and a shot glass. No one in the building had a whole bottle of the stuff, but everyone volunteered to help fill one good-sized bottle. When they got to the Russian checkpoint the guard on duty let them pass without incident because they were just a group of women and children.

About fifteen minutes later they arrived at the converted school. Inside they found a single guard sitting behind a dilapidated desk. My mother started to talk to him, but of course the man had no idea what she was saying. Then she started to cry, which immediately caused the overtired children to also cry. That alarmed the guard, who began gesturing wildly for them to calm down. About then my mother pulled out the shot glass and poured the guard a drink. He downed it in a flash. Once she had his attention, Resi started to negotiate.

Using sign language, my mother somehow conveyed to him that all of these children, plus the baby she was carrying, belonged to someone in his custody. She handed the guard a piece of paper with my father's name on it and got him to understand that she would give him the entire bottle of booze if he would produce her husband. When the guard hesitated, she started to cry again, which got the kids crying again too. While all this crying was going on, Hanna Schmidt took the bottle of Schnapps from my mother and poured the guard two more shots, which he downed in quick succession. This greatly improved his mood.

To my mother's total amazement, the guard got up and walked off with the piece of paper. After several agonizing minutes he returned with my father in tow. While Hanna was handing over the bottle, my mother pushed her dazed husband out the door. Hanna sprinted after them with the crying children. Then they all ran like hell.

When they reached the bridge, the new guard on duty waved them through without asking to see their papers. He was probably simply not in the mood to deal with a bunch of crying kids. They only slowed down once they were back in the American zone. My mother said that all of them were crying by that point, including my father. It was their way of releasing the terrible tension of the last few hours. It had been the closest of close calls.

Heinrich spent the next several weeks deeply depressed. Of all the awful things he'd experienced during the war, that incident was the one that left him with the most serious case of post-traumatic stress. For weeks he had a recurring nightmare in which he was chained to the wall of a dark cave. Night after night, that dream had him in a cold sweat. The other thing that tormented him was the thought of what had happened to the rest of the men in that room. Three of them had been young lads who reminded him very much of the boys from his Czech base. One of them had looked eerily like Wilhelm. He spent hours thinking about what those youngsters were going to have to endure in that wretched mine: how their young lives had basically been stolen from them. Needless to say, he never set foot in the Russian zone again.

There are no good estimates of exactly how many innocent civilians the Soviet occupiers kidnapped inside their newly acquired territories. They had already enslaved 500,000 German and Austrian soldiers. Perhaps they thought, why not add a few hundred thousand more slaves? The Russians probably felt entitled to kidnap Germans and Austrians since the Nazis had instigated the war that had taken the lives of more than 30 million Russians, including nine million of their children. They probably reasoned that since the war had severely damaged their economy, making the enemy pay them back through forced labor was justified. Whatever the rationale, the abduction of innocent citizens in the post-war period was a horrendous act perpetrated against an already defeated peoples.

My father eventually recovered from this latest ordeal. When I asked him how he was able to keep going despite the hardships, he stoically said that there simply was no other choice. He had a family to care for so he got on with it. He revived his auto repair business at a new location, although the Americans no longer brought him work. Most US troops had long since returned to the States. He kept working at his small enterprise for the next several years although he barely made enough money to support his family.

On April 10, 1948, the Dolezal family experienced the joy of welcoming a new life. Herman Dolezal was a robust baby with rosy cheeks, brown eyes and straight brown hair. Everyone remarked at how much he resembled his father. My mother had sailed through the delivery even though it took place at home, with only the help of a neighbor. Linz still lacked a functioning hospital, and doctors were impossible to find.

For three months after Herman's birth everything seemed fine. Resi felt well and was enjoying motherhood. Walter was doing really well at his new managerial job and had a lovely new girlfriend. Elisabeth was busy serving a growing number of customers and my father's former business partners had returned all of the money he had deposited with them. Then little Herman became ill. At first it was just a fever. His umbilical cord had been slightly inflamed ever since he was born, most likely because of conditions connected with his home birth. What no one realized was that his fever was a sign that he'd developed sepsis. Soon he was having trouble breathing and began lapsing in and out of consciousness.

Heinrich and Walter frantically searched the city for medical help. My father knew that Herman needed penicillin, but simply couldn't find any. Linz had lost its hospitals to bombs. A few small clinics had been established, but even they had no penicillin. He approached the American base, which had a small hospital and asked if he might bring his son there. They turned him down. With so many people in need, they simply couldn't help everyone. He even tried the Black Market. For days their neighbors shared every home remedy they'd ever heard of, in the hopes of helping the baby recover. It was all in vain. Three months after his birth, little Herman died. My mother found him cold in his crib.

My brother's death was only mentioned on two occasions and only because I asked about conditions after the war. Otherwise, neither of my parents ever spoke about the loss of their only son: their silence an indication of the depth of their pain. The only anecdote I was ever able to uncover about what happened after his passing came from my grandmother Elisabeth. When I was seventeen we went to Austria for a family visit. One day she and I were alone in her apartment and I asked her about that infamous copy of *Mein Kampf*. I was hoping that she still had it and that she might let me take a look. That's when she told me what my father did to the book.

After Herman's death he had become extremely despondent. Then he became furiously angry. After considerable thought he concluded that the misery experienced by his family, including the death of his son, was the fault of one person: Adolph Hitler. He reasoned that without Hitler's total insanity, the war would never have escalated into a world-wide catastrophe. If the war had been more limited, the country would not have been in ruins. Hospitals and clinics would have been open. Then his wife would have been able to give birth in sanitary conditions and Herman would have been able to receive any medical attention he might have needed. Was Adolph Hitler really the cause of my brother's death? Not directly of course, but to my grief-stricken father, the blame ran straight to his door.

In that state of mind, Heinrich searched the dining room bureau to find his signed copy of *Mein Kampf:* the book he'd once so proudly shown off to everyone. He marched it down the stairs and over to his shop. There he lit his Bunsen Burner and, starting with the autographed page, burned one page after another until the entire book had been reduced to ashes. When he was done, he shredded the extravagant leather cover and threw it into the trash. That act of destruction didn't fix anything, but it did allow him to symbolically vent his frustration and anger at what the Nazi's had done to his family.

Despite all of the challenges, the Dolezal family carried on. My father continued to earn just enough from his repair business to keep his family fed. By contrast, Walter did very well at his new job and soon married his fiancé, the lovely Paulina. Because of his excellent salary they were able to rent an apartment of their own. In June of 1949 they welcomed their first child, a daughter they named Renate. I was born one year later on May 16, 1950.

Although neither of my parents ever said it, I always wondered if they hadn't been hoping for a son to fill the void left by the death of my brother. Instead they got another girl and a very different girl from their first daughter. My sister Elfrieda had a lovely olive complexion, brown eyes and a head full of dark curls. She definitely took after the Romanian side of the family. In contrast, I was slight, pale, blue eyed and had straight blond hair. Clearly I was from the Czech and Austrian part of the gene pool. The two of us could not have been more different. Our differences weren't just physical either. Throughout our lives we always had completely different interests, habits and temperaments. Despite those differences we were great companions throughout our childhood.

Although life in Linz continued to improve, my parents had already resolved to leave. Whenever I asked them about their motivations, the same two reasons were given: the economy and the Russians. Although basic services had been restored, everyday commodities were still in short supply, even basic food stuffs. The other shortage was housing. Some rebuilding had begun, but my father was never able to find an apartment for our family. So, we continued to live with Grandma in her badly overcrowded flat on Bethlehemstrasse.

The Russians were the other big factor. They'd recently dropped a terrible iron curtain between east and west. Although we lived in the western part of the country my father was always afraid that they might somehow engineer a takeover of the whole country. He'd seen enough of their behavior and simply did not trust them. He told me that his strongest motivation for leaving

Europe was to get as far from them as possible. After considerable discussion my parents decided that our family needed to go to the only place that was both far away and trustworthy: America.

Beginning in 1951 my parents applied annually to enter the United States. Every year they were denied because that year's quota for Austrian immigrants had been reached. This went on for three years. One day my father was standing outside the US consulate in Linz waiting to hear if our names had made the latest list. He'd been there for hours. Finally, a young man came out to read the names of the chosen few. Our names were not among them. The young man then declared all other applications void for the remainder of the year. Almost as an afterthought, he mentioned that the Canadians had recently created more openings for immigrants from Austria. Then he gave their address. My father started to run. When he reached the Canadians, they immediately let him in and gave him forms to complete. One week later he saw our names posted on their bulletin board. We were to become Canadians!

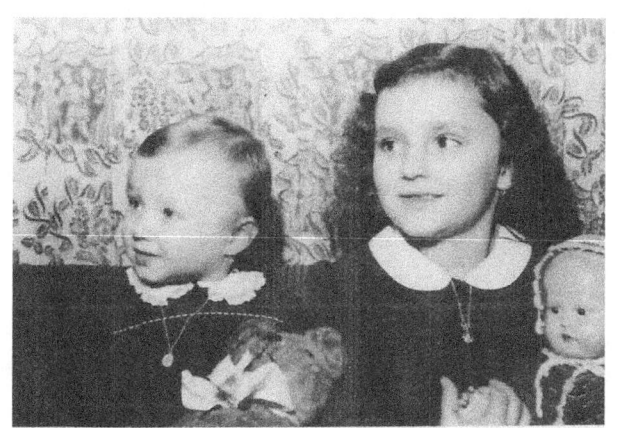

Elfi and Me, 1952, Linz

Elfi and Me, 1954, Linz

Chapter 13
Oh Canada!

In May of 1954 my parents began preparing to leave Austria for good. My father was 36, my mother was 31, my sister was nine and I was four. I can't imagine what was going through my parents' minds as they got ready to move to a country they'd never seen and where people spoke a language they didn't understand. By then, the final toll of the war had been fully calculated. My parents had lost well over a decade of their young lives to endless anxiety and grief. My father had never been able to find anyone from his father's family, nor did he ever again hear from any of the boys, although they were probably alive and well somewhere in the country. In addition, Heinrich had lost every one of his childhood friends and my mother had lost six of her seven brothers. And of course, they had also lost their only son.

My strongest memory of our family's preparations to leave was my grandmother carefully folding American money into strips which she then sewed into the seams and lapels of my parent's clothing. A good move considering that the crew on our ship broke into our trunks and stole everything of value. Over the years my father had somehow managed to accumulate about eight hundred American dollars. Not a lot of money for an expedition to the other side of the globe, but enough to get started.

My parents had originally planned to settle in Montreal because that's where we disembarked, but the language barrier turned out to be too great. Heinrich had been working hard to learn a bit of English, only to discover that Montreal was predominantly French speaking. After a couple of frustrating days, we boarded a train to Toronto. Sometime later that day, I remember sitting on the porch of a house while my father spoke to the owner about renting the top floor. The house was owned by a boisterous Sicilian clan consisting of four adults and five children. None of the Italians spoke English and my father spoke only German, so I have no idea how they managed to seal the deal. He probably just kept laying dollar bills on the table until the landlord nodded his head. Despite the language barrier, we lived harmoniously upstairs from those hard-working people for over two years.

Heinrich landed a job on his second day in Toronto. When I asked him how he managed to find work so quickly and without any English, he said that he simply showed prospective employers his tools. It seems that they only needed to take one look at his custom-made shears to know that he was capable of doing the work. During our years in Canada he worked first at an autobody shop, then at a large outfit that made stainless steel hospital kitchens and finally for the Toronto Transit Commission. He was never unemployed. My father was one of those people who managed to work his way through life regardless of the circumstances.

In 1956 we heard the shocking news that the Russians had departed Austria. This was unprecedented and totally unexpected. Austria was the only territory that the Russians ever gave up voluntarily. They hung on to all of their other satellites until 1991 when the Soviet Union finally collapsed. The story of why they left is a complex mix of political wrangling, economic failure and total rejection by the Austrian people, who were completely fed up with the behavior of the Russians.

My father admitted that he was stunned to hear that the Soviets had given up their Austrian territories. Years later I asked him if their withdrawal ever made him regret his decision to emigrate. He said that it had not. The reason he gave was that Canada had made us feel welcome from the very first day we arrived. He pointed out that at no time did anyone ever comment on his being Austrian or rebuke him for having served in Hitler's army. Canadians had been unfailingly kind and polite to us even during the years right after the war. That benevolent acceptance included the Canadian family just down the street, who'd lost their only son in that terrible conflict. Our family was always deeply grateful to Canadians for their tolerance and open-mindedness.

We'd only been in Toronto for about two years when my parents bought an old Victorian row house. Immigrants know the value of having a roof over their heads, so they always buy a house as soon as they can, even if it means having tenants. For years we lived on the ground floor and put up with the inconvenience of having tenants on the second and third floors. Ten years after we arrived in Canada we were living tenant free in a nice house, in a pleasant Toronto suburb. A decade or so after that, we also owned a cottage on a beautiful lake northeast of the city. We were an immigrant success story!

None of it had been easy though. My main recollection of my parent's lives during my childhood was that they were always working. They both had jobs and sometimes even worked on weekends. The first time our family visited a cottage on a northern lake was because my parents had been hired to paint the cabin's interior. Several other people on the lake subsequently hired my parents to do the same for them. That enabled us to spend time in beautiful lake country. My sister and I probably thought that we were on vacation as we played in the water without a care in the world. Meanwhile our parents were inside working hard to earn a few extra dollars.

Although we were never a wealthy family, my sister and I had every advantage. The schools in Ontario were excellent and they provided us both with a wonderful education. From our very first year in Canada my parents always managed to make our Christmases special. Elfi and I quickly amassed every toy imaginable. It was a wonderful childhood.

The most important thing that my father had wanted for his family was peace. That had been his motivation for leaving Europe. He'd seen more than enough of hatred and destruction and wanted my sister and me to grow up without fear and oppression. In Canada we found peace, prosperity and so much more.

Our Family After the War

Boarding Pass 1954, Rotterdam, Holland

Elfi and Me 1955, Toronto

Walter and Paulina Wedding Portrait

Heinrich and Ingrid 1957, Toronto

Heinrich and Ingrid 1959, Toronto

Elfrieda at Eighteen, Toronto

Celebrating 25 Years Married

Elisabeth at Age 89

Grandma Piribauer at Age 92

Ingrid, Heinrich and Elfi 1992, Toronto

Linda and Lisa with Grampa Dolezal

Heinrich and Theresa 1985

Chapter 14
Post Script

During the next few decades our family story was one of assimilation and success. At eighteen Elfrieda met and married the love of her life. They soon had two wonderful daughters, whom they named Linda and Lisa. Both of these remarkable women attended university and pursued successful careers. They now have families of their own and I know that my parents would have been very proud of the success of their four great-grandchildren, who have all either graduated from university or about to do so.

I chose a different path. Instead of marrying at a young age I stayed with my studies and eventually achieved a post-graduate degree from the University of Toronto. After working for the Ontario Government as a community development officer, I launched my own consulting firm in the field of Organization Development. This work took me all over the world. I remember looking out my airplane window as we landed in Shanghai and wondering what my maternal grandmother would have thought about my life. She'd lived so simply in her rural village. Would she have even been able to comprehend how much the world changed in the decades after the war? I'm guessing that she wouldn't have been able to imagine that a female grandchild of hers would have her own business and be taken seriously by large corporations.

There were so many ironies in my parent's lives, not the least of which was how each of them died. In the summer of 1988 my parents went to Austria for a six-week family visit. They spent their first week in Linz, then traveled all around Austria with Walter and his wife Paulina. I received several letters, accompanied by snap shots of the happy foursome. In one of her letters my mother commented on the fact that she and my father had finally been able to visit all of the places in Austria that neither of them had ever seen before.

My parents spent the last week of their vacation in my mother's hometown of Breitenau. On their first night in the village, her sister Hilda hosted a backyard party that the entire community attended. It was a joyous event that enabled my mother to reconnect with many of her relatives and childhood friends. I have a photo of her from that night. In that picture she looks totally happy, drinking wine and chatting with old acquaintances, under a canopy of grape vines. After that reunion, she went to bed in the house where she'd been born and died in her sleep. A massive heart attack took her life in the middle of the night.

Theresa Piribauer Dolezal had been born in Breitenau 65 years earlier, but had only lived in her home town for about eighteen years. She spent majority of the life in Canada. Because she died in Breitenau, her funeral service was held in the same church in which she'd been baptized. Talk about coming full circle. It almost seems as though it was her destiny to return to her native soil for her final rest. My sister and I were shocked and grief stricken at her sudden passing. Our only consolation was that she'd been with so many of the people she loved before she died.

My father's death was equally ironic in that he was eventually killed by the very thing that had saved him during the war. His salvation, and the salvation of his descendants, had been that he was a talented metal worker. That skill had kept him far from the fighting. Unfortunately, a lifetime of inhaling metal fumes eventually developed into a deadly case of Lymphoma. He passed peacefully in 1996 at the age of 78. My sister and I were by his side.

The last thing he said to us was that we weren't to take his death too hard. Right to the end he was thinking of others. He also said that he was content and that he'd had a happy life. If my father was able to say that after everything he'd endured, what possible complaint can the rest of us have?

Chapter 15
Personal Reflections

I embarked on the journey into my family's war experiences because I needed to know if my beloved father had secretly been some sort of Nazi monster. To my great relief, I learned that he not only never engaged in any sort of violence, but that he'd always conducted himself with bravery and honor. He helped to save the lives of the young boys in his care and diligently took care of the people in his household. Throughout it all, he never lost sight of what was important—his humanity and civility.

My mother was the other strong person in the family. I simply can't imagine how she managed to keep going during those horrendous last years of the war when the bombs were falling all around. I doubt that I have the grit to withstand what she and my father endured. They will always be my heroes, for their bravery and their determination to create a better life for their children.

I also learned a valuable lesson about war—namely that all sides lose. That was certainly true of WWII, in which even the victors lost vast numbers of people, money and equipment, not to mention the emotional anguish of the families who lost loved ones. Of course, the ultimate price was paid by the people of Europe. They lost their lives in the millions and saw their cities reduced to ash. While they were cheering for the Nazis in the 1930s, Germans and Austrians could never have imagined that their world was about to be completely destroyed. In the end, those who called most vociferously for the death and destruction of others, led their own people to that exact fate.

The great gift of history is its ability to teach us lessons. In the case of World War II, it's vital to understand that the naked aggression of the Nazis was deliberately engineered and then sold to the public. Apologists for the German-speaking nations have suggested that no one in Austria or Germany ever wanted the wholesale destruction of Europe. They've argued that the public simply wanted to restore their homeland. These apologists have gone on to say that the general public never knew the full extent of the horrors being perpetrated in the concentration camps. These are poor excuses.

The truth is that Adolph Hitler clearly laid out his message of race hatred in his book *Mein Kampf*. Millions of Germans and Austrians read his words. For at least a decade, the public knew that elimination of other nationalities was one of the guiding principles of Nazism. Hitler spoke openly about his intention to obliterate entire groups. In fact, he shouted his message of murder and mayhem from every available podium.

The war and the resultant destruction of both Germany and Austria must continue to be lessons for all of us. We should never imagine that it was too long ago or that it can't possibly happen again. In fact, conflict is guaranteed whenever the public allows itself to be seduced by the message that it's us against them—that some people are worthy, while others are disposable.

While it may have been difficult to stand up to the Nazis once they'd gained full control, people could have refused to vote for Hitler in the first place. They could have stayed away from his rallies. Empty stadiums and deserted streets would have sent a strong message. Instead, they listened to his hateful rants and cheered. This underscores the fact that supporting leaders who diminish whole groups of people inevitably leads to senseless bloodshed.

After the war, Germans and Austrians acknowledged their complicity in Hitler's campaign of hatred and genocide. They faced the criminal history of their fathers and grandfathers. In the ensuing years, both nations did an excellent job of teaching the next generation that racism is disgraceful. One campaign, dubbed *Neimals Vergessen (Never Forget)*, helped educate the public about the need to reject leaders who incite violence. This is a message that we need to pay attention to again since the purveyors of mass murder are once again up to their old tricks.

At the time of this writing, Russia has invaded Ukraine. This is an unprovoked and deliberately brutal attack on civilians. Over the decades, the citizens of Europe had lulled themselves into thinking that a war couldn't possibly take place on their soil again. There was even talk of disbanding NATO. Today we're once again seeing horrendous scenes of senseless destruction and people running for their lives. Once again, a psychopath has brainwashed an entire population with poisonous lies. Once again, innocent youths like my father are being sent to the front under a false pretext.

Part of the reason for this sad state of affairs is that the Russian state made a major error after World War II. They never acknowledged, or atoned for, their many reprehensible actions during that war. They never openly admitted that Stalin killed and deported millions of innocent civilians. They never apologized to the hundreds of thousands of people they enslaved in their gulags. Nor did they ever admit that they oppressed the people living in their satellites throughout the Soviet era. Instead, they created a false narrative of themselves as the aggrieved party. They told themselves the lie that they were the victims and that they had scores to settle. In this frame of mind, they invented the justification for their current brutality.

Just before the invasion of Ukraine, Russian citizens overwhelmingly supported the annexation of that country. The public bought into Putin's absurd propaganda that Ukraine didn't exist as a true nation—that the Ukrainians needed to be liberated and brought back into the fold. That's exactly what the Nazis told their people when they rationalized the takeover of Austria and the Czech provinces. Soon, the Russian people will learn what the Germans and Austrians learned sixty years ago—that it was all a lie. Young conscripts will realize that they've been sent to the killing fields and that their leaders don't care if they ever return to their families. At home, sanctions are shredding their economy. As their standard of living crumbles around them, Russian citizens will finally come to understand that they too are the victims of Putin's war. The freedoms and economic gains that took six decades to achieve will vanish before their eyes.

Today, brave Russians are risking their lives to protest the criminal actions of their state. Tomorrow we may find ourselves in the streets doing exactly the same thing. That's because millions of people in our own country are being brainwashed on a daily basis. Purveyors of grievance and hatred are busy convincing millions of Americans that they too are victims and that there are enemies everywhere. Shockingly, these enemies include their fellow citizens. A key lesson of both World War II and the current war in Ukraine is that normal, everyday citizens can be swayed to support violence. Our only salvation is a deep commitment to democracy and freedom of speech, and a firm belief in the dignity of all human beings.

> *"Those who can make you believe absurdities*
> *can make you commit atrocities."*
> *Voltaire*

Author Bio

Ingrid Bens is a certified professional facilitator and the president of Facilitation Tutor, a consulting firm created to further the practice of facilitation as a core leadership competency. Ingrid has a Master's Degree in Adult Education and over 25 years of experience as an Organization Development consultant.

Ingrid Bens is the author of multiple bestselling books on the topic of facilitation. The most notable of these is *Facilitating with Ease!* which is in its fourth edition. She is also the author of several textbooks about conflict management and teamwork. She is retired in Sarasota, Florida.

Sources

This is not a history book, although it does attempt to narrate as accurately as possible the lives of my family and the many people they encountered. Please note that all family names cited in this book are real, but that all other names are fictitious. Most of what's in these pages is drawn from the stories that my parents told. Other information was gathered from research into both historical data and from reading the memoirs of those who survived World War II. The internet has recently revolutionized our access to information about the past. In particular I recommend viewing the many excellent videos about that conflict that are available on both Netflix and YouTube.

Articles

Hahn, Robert. "What Happened at Linz." *The American Scholar*. April 2021.

Books

Albright, Madeleine. *Prague Winter: A Personal Story of Remembrance and War 1937.* Harper Collins. New York, NY. 2012.

Craig, William. *Enemy at the Gates: The Battle for Stalingrad.* Open Road Integrated Media. New York, NY, 2015.

Lucas, James. *War on the Eastern Front: The German Soldier in Russia 1941-1945.* Cooper and Lucas Ltd. New York, NY. 2020.

Kershaw. Ian. *The End: The Defiance and Destruction of Hitler's Germany 1944-1945.* Gildan Media Corp. 2011.

MacDonoch, Giles. *After the Reich. The Brutal History of the Allied Occupation.* Perseus Books Group. New York, NY. 2007.

Neuman, Ariana. *When Time Stopped. A Memoir of My Father's War and What Remains.* Simon and Schuster. New York, NY. 2020.

O'Neil, Bill. *The World War 2 Trivia Book.* LAK Publishing. New York, NY. 2017.

Overly, Richard, ed. *Complete World War II. 1939–1945.* The New York Times. New York, NY. 2013.

Rothkirchen, Livia. *The Jews of Bohemia and Moravia: Facing the Holocaust,.* University of Nebraska Press, Lincoln, NE. 2005.

Rozell, Mathew. *The Things our Fathers Saw.* Woodchuck Hollow, Press, Hartford, CT. 2015.

Scheiderbauer, Armin. *Adventures of My Youth: A German Soldier on the Eastern Front.* Helion and Company. Warwick, UK. 2003.

Shirer, William. *The Rise and Fall of the Third Reich*. Simon and Shuster. New York, NY. 2011.

Sturgeon, Alison, ed. *World War II. The Definitive Visual History.* DK Books. New York, NY. 2009.

Netflix Videos*

World War II in Color. (2019) Netflix. Episode 5 - Siege of Stalingrad.

World War II in Color. (2019) Netflix. Episode 7 - Battle of the Bulge.

Hitler: A Career. Netflix. Joachim Fest.

Internet Searches*

Allied-Occupied Austria: Wikipedia

Anschluss: Wikipedia

Military Production in WW II

Number of Soldiers in WW II

War Damage in Austria

Worldwide Deaths in World War II

YouTube Videos*

Germany 1945: Restored Footage - George Stevens, May 2020

Germany Invades Austria - Periscope Film, March 2020

German Troops March into Austria – British Pathé, April 2014

Hitler: Germany's Fatal Attraction – Timeline World History, Jan 2021

How the Nazi Party Began (Germany's Fatal Attraction) Timeline World History, January 2020

How and Why Hitler and His Cohorts Made Strategic Mistakes. David Hoffman, September 2017

Nazi Germany: Pictures of Madness, 1937 -1939, Chronos Media,

Post War Austria from Occupation to Independence. David Hoffman, January 2019

Why Germans Followed Hitler. David Hoffman, January 2019

World War II Explained. The Life Guide, January 2021

*Note that online videos and internet search terms change constantly. The titles cited above can quickly become outdated since the content on internet sites is continuously being updated and amended.

Special thanks to cousin Walter Dolezal Jr. who spent years researching and recreating the detailed genealogy of the Dolezal clan.

Modern Day Linz, Austria

www.ingramcontent.com/pod-product-compliance
Lightning Source LLC
Chambersburg PA
CBHW070603010526
44118CB00012B/1434